STAND FIRM IN THE FAITH

An Exposition of II Corinthians

Robert Gromacki

BAKER BOOK HOUSE
Grand Rapids, Michigan

ISBN: 0-8010-3730-1

**Library of Congress Catalog Card
Number: 78-068055**

PHOTOLITHOPRINTED BY CUSHING - MALLOY, INC.
ANN ARBOR, MICHIGAN, UNITED STATES OF AMERICA
1978

To these
faithful pastors
who have ministered
to my family and to me

William Broughton
Dale Cadman
Hall Dautel
Albert Eisenhart
Robert Gilbert
Paul Jackson
Robert McMillan
John Teeters

Contents

Illustrations

Preface

To study the epistle of II Corinthians in detail is extremely profitable. It has enriched my life, both as a believer and as a preacher of the gospel. I am convinced that no one should undertake the ministry of the oral proclamation of divine truth, whether from the pulpit or in a Bible class, without some intimate knowledge of this epistle. It provides rich insights into the heart and mind of Paul. His purposes and motivations shine forth. It strips away the facade of outward appearance with which so many Christians are impressed. This epistle will cause you to take a fresh look at both yourself and your service for Christ.

This study has been designed to teach the Word of God to others. It is an attempt to make clear the meaning of the English text (King James Version) through organization, exposition, and careful usage of the Greek text. It is planned as a readable study through a nontechnical vocabulary and smooth transition from one section to another.

Divided into thirteen chapters, it can be used by adult Sunday school classes or Bible study groups for a traditional quarter of thirteen weeks. Also, it can be adapted easily into a six-month study by devoting two sessions to each chapter. Concluding each chapter are discussion questions, designed to stimulate personal inquiry and to make the truth of God relevant. This book, in addition, can be used by one person as a private Bible study guide. In either case, this exposition should be read with an open Bible. It is the author's prayer that men and women will be blessed and edified as they undertake this study of II Corinthians.

A special word of thanks is extended to Cornelius Zylstra, editor of Baker Book House, who encouraged me to undertake this project. This volume will complement my exposition of I Corinthians, entitled *Called to Be Saints,* also published by Baker Book House. Also, my love and appreciation go to my wife, Gloria, who carefully typed the manuscript.

Introduction

I. WRITER

Few have disputed the Pauline character or authorship of this book. The author definitely identifies himself as Paul (1:1; 10:1). Many of the historical allusions within the book coincide with our knowledge of Paul's life contained elsewhere in Acts and in other epistles. For instance, Timothy, Silas, and Titus were numbered among his associates (1:1, 19; 2:13; 7:6, 13–14; 8:6). His geographical movements and planned trips harmonize with Paul's itinerary (1:16; 2:12; 7:5). Some of his personal experiences, including that of his dramatic escape from Damascus, can be found in Acts (11:32–33; cf. Acts 9:24–25). It is true that much of the autobiographical data is not contained in Paul's other letters or in Acts, but this should not be construed as an argument against his authorship. Would a forger have included so much personal data not found elsewhere nor known by many if he wanted to pass off the book as a Pauline original? Only the one who in fact had experienced these events could report them publicly. The book opens with a typical Pauline greeting and blessing of grace and peace (1:2; cf. I Cor. 1:3; Gal. 1:3; Eph. 1:2).

II. CITY OF CORINTH

Corinth was located on a narrow strip of land, called an isthmus, connecting the Peloponnesus with northern Greece. This isthmus also formed the land bridge between the Aegean and the Adriatic seas. Located forty miles west of Athens, Corinth was the capital of this southern province called Achaia. The Romans had destroyed the city in 146 B.C., but because its location was so important, they later rebuilt it under Julius Caesar in 46 B.C. By the time Paul arrived in the city (A.D. 50–52), the city had grown to a population of 500,000. Today only the ruins of the city remain.

In that day Corinth was the crossroads for travel and commerce, both north and south for the Greek peninsula and east and west between Rome and the Near East. It had two seaports, Cenchrea on the Aegean Sea to the east and Lechaeum on the edge of the Gulf of Corinth to the west. Commercial ships, instead of sailing around the dangerous southern tip of Greece, were portaged across the isthmus from one port to the other. This saved time and was less risky. Thus Corinth became a city of wealth and pleasure. People went there with money to spend and to indulge themselves in varied pleasures.

On the highest point in the city stood the pagan temple of Aphrodite, the goddess of love, full of religious prostitutes to serve the wishes of its devotees. These women also participated in the night life of the city. Also located at Corinth was a stadium where athletic contests, next best to the Greek Olympics, were held every two years. Although Corinth was influenced by the philosophy of Athens, it never became a center of intellectual learning. The citizens and the tourists were too busy making and spending money to do much rationalistic speculation. Because it was a mercantile center, all kinds of people settled there:

The Canal of Corinth

Romans, Greeks, and Jews. Corinth became a cosmopolitan city with all of the attending vices attached to that type of society.

III. ESTABLISHMENT OF THE CHURCH

The founding of the Corinthian church was recorded by Luke in Acts (18:1–18). From Athens Paul had sent his associates Silas and Timothy back to the Macedonian churches at Philippi, Thessalonica, and Berea (Acts 17:15–16; cf. I Thess. 3:1–6), which were started earlier on this same (second) missionary journey. When Paul therefore left Athens for Corinth, he went alone. Cut off from his friends and supporting churches, Paul worked at tentmaking, a craft he had learned as a youth, to meet his financial needs. He found both work and lodging with a Jewish couple, Aquila and Priscilla, who practiced this same craft and who had been expelled from Rome because of the anti-Semitic decree of Caesar Claudius. Perhaps through personal conversation with Paul and his subsequent synagogue preaching, this couple came to know Jesus Christ as their Messiah and Savior.

During the week, Paul worked with his hands, but every Sabbath he was in the synagogue, logically proving from the Old Testament that the promised Messiah had to suffer death and be raised from the dead and that Jesus was indeed that promised Savior (cf. Acts 17:2–3). Many in attendance, both Jews and Gentile proselytes to the Jewish religion, were convinced and believed. When Silas and Timothy joined Paul at Corinth with a good report of the faith and stedfastness of the Macedonian Christians, Paul was constrained to press the claims of Jesus Christ even more strongly upon his synagogue listeners. When this occurred, the Jews resisted and blasphemed, forcing Paul to leave the synagogue with this declaration: "Your blood

Paul's Second Missionary Journey

be upon your own heads; I am clean; from henceforth I will go unto the Gentiles" (Acts 18:6). It was also about this time that Paul wrote I Thessalonians, based upon the content of Timothy's report.

Paul then moved his ministry into the house of Justus, which was adjacent to the Jewish synagogue. Soon after, the chief ruler of the synagogue, Crispus, along with his family, believed. From this new site, a ministry to the pagan, idolatrous Corinthians was begun with much success. The opposition must have been intense at that time because Paul received special encouragement from God. He was informed that he would not suffer bodily harm and that many would be converted through his ministry. Paul then labored for eighteen months (A.D. 50–52) both as an evangelist and as a teacher of the new congregation.

In the midst of his ministry at Corinth, the Jews brought charges against Paul before Gallio, the political deputy or proconsul of Achaia (Acts 18:12–17). Since the accusations were religious and not political in nature, Gallio refused to arbitrate the matter. In driving the Jews from the judgment seat, Gallio declared the innocence of Paul and recognized the troublesome character of the Jews. Later, the Gentile proselytes to Judaism smote Sosthenes, the chief ruler of the synagogue, who probably was a Gentile himself and a recent convert to Christianity; again, Gallio reacted negatively.

Even after this burst of persecution, Paul remained a "good while" in Corinth. With Aquila and Priscilla he then left Corinth and set sail for Antioch in Syria via Ephesus.

IV. TIME AND PLACE

Paul left Aquila and Priscilla at Ephesus and sailed for Caesarea (Acts 18:18–22). On his arrival he visited the Jerusalem church and then returned to his home church at

Antioch. After spending "some time" there, he departed, and went over all the country of Galatia and Phrygia in order, strengthening all the disciples (18:23). Thus began his third missionary journey.

During Paul's absence from Ephesus, Apollos, an eloquent Jewish teacher of the doctrine of John the Baptist, came to that city and was led to a knowledge of Christ by Aquila and Priscilla. With his new faith, Apollos traveled to Corinth in Achaia where he was received by the Corinthian believers and where he had a successful public ministry among the Jews (Acts 18:24–28).

While Apollos was in Corinth, Paul reached Ephesus where he would minister for the next three years (A.D. 52–55; Acts 19:1–10; 20:31). About this time, because of increasing factionalism in the Corinthian church, Apollos left that city and returned to Ephesus (I Cor. 1:12; 16:12). Some have suggested that Paul made a quick, personal visit to Corinth to arbitrate the controversy but was unsuccessful (II Cor. 2:1; 12:14). Although this cannot be documented, it may have taken place. Since Corinth was only two hundred miles west across the Aegean Sea from Ephesus, travel and communication between the two cities was comparatively easy.

The situation at Corinth continued to deteriorate. Members of the household of Chloe brought a firsthand report of the divisions within the assembly (I Cor. 1:11). They were followed by three members of the Corinthian church (Stephanas, Fortunatus, and Achaicus), who brought Paul a financial gift (16:17). Perhaps they also carried to Paul a letter from the church in which questions were asked about various doctrinal and moral issues (7:1). Thus, through personal conversations with Apollos, the Chloe household, and the three church emissaries plus the content of the letter, Paul learned about the troubled state of the Corinthian church. Unable to leave Ephesus at that time (16:3–9), Paul wrote I Corinthians to resolve the many problems. It was probably written near the end of his ministry at Ephesus since he had already made plans for leaving the province of Asia (16:5–7). Therefore it was composed during the fall or winter of A.D. 55 because he said that he would stay at Ephesus until Pentecost.

Paul remained at Ephesus after the writing of I Corinthians to continue his ministry in that city and to await the results of his authoritative letter. Paul had hoped that the double thrust of the letter and of Timothy's visit (I Cor. 16:10–11) would solve the difficulties at Corinth, but apparently they did not. The intense church factions and growing opposition to Paul's apostolic authority persisted.

The Marble Street, at Ephesus

Taking matters into his own hands, Paul probably made a trip across the Aegean Sea to Corinth to resolve the matters himself. Although this trip was unrecorded in Acts, the anticipated third trip (12:14; 13:1–2) presupposes a second trip made between the original journey to evangelize and the writing of II Corinthians. This hasty visit ended in failure. Paul retreated once more to Ephesus with insults of his person and rejections of his authority ringing in his ears and burdening his heart (2:1; 12:14, 21; 13:1–2). False Jewish apostles had attacked Paul's integrity (chapters 10–11), and the sinning members were still unrepentant (12:21). Paul decided that he would not return to Corinth until the Corinthians adopted a different attitude toward him (1:23).

There is some speculation that Paul wrote a brief letter to Corinth at this time in criticism of the person who was against him (2:5–10; 7:12). Since there is no objective, manuscript evidence for the existence of this letter, it would be regarded as another lost letter, making two altogether (cf. I Cor. 5:9). Support for this lost letter is based upon Paul's statement: "For out of much affliction and anguish of heart I wrote unto you with many tears" (2:4; cf. 7:8). Could this tearful letter be identified with the first epistle or is it an epistolary aorist reference to the second epistle itself? Most say not and conclude that this letter is now lost. Many liberals say that this letter was incorporated into our present second epistle as chapters ten through thirteen, but there is no objective support for such a position. At this time Titus did leave Paul for Corinth, and if such a letter did exist, he probably took it with him (7:8–13).

Because of increased pressure at Ephesus, Paul went to Troas where he expected to find Titus waiting for him (2:12–13), but his associate was not there. Burdened over his absence, Paul moved on to Macedonia, possibly to Philippi. Here Paul encountered more troubles (7:5), but he was comforted when Titus came with a glowing report from Corinth (7:6–16). Revival had broken out and the church was again warm and responsive toward Paul. He thus was prompted to write to inform them of his rejoicing over the repentance of the majority, his continued concern over the benevolent collection, and his sorrow over the constant opposition of the few. He therefore wrote from Macedonia about A.D. 55 in preparation for his visit to Achaia and to Corinth (cf. Acts 20:2).

V. PURPOSES

The purposes behind the writing of the book are inseparably connected with the historical background of the epistle. He thus wrote to present the purpose of his sufferings in Asia, notably at Ephesus (1:3–11); to explain why he changed his plans for a return visit to Corinth (1:12–2:4); to give instructions about the discipline and the reconciliation of the offender (2:5–11); to express his joy over the revival (2:12–13; cf. 7:15–16); to set forth the superiority of the ministry of grace to that of law (2:14–6:10); to appeal for separation from false teachers (6:11–7:16); to urge the church to fulfill its collection responsibility (8:1–9:15); and to vindicate his apostleship against the charges of false apostles (10:1–13:14).

VI. DISTINCTIVE FEATURES

This is the most autobiographical of all Paul's epistles. It gives an insight into the personal life and ministry of the apostle that none of the other letters gives. Because of the false charges made against him, Paul was forced against his personal wishes to reveal events and secrets unknown to most of his converts. He prefaced his disclosures with these words:

> I say again, Let no man think me a fool; if otherwise, yet as a fool receive me, that I may boast myself a little. That which I speak, I speak it not after the Lord, but as it were foolishly, in this confidence of boasting (11:16–17).

Over and over again he inserted self-conscious explanations: "I speak as a fool" (11:21, 23) and "I must needs glory" (11:18, 30; 12:1, 5, 6). He concluded: "I am become a fool in glorying; ye have compelled me" (12:11). These expedient disclosures reveal that Paul suffered far more for the cause of Christ than any man would imagine. His sufferings became his main defense against the unjust charges. What had his enemies suffered for Christ? That was his countercharge.

The book also reveals the warm, human character of Paul. Many have pictured Paul as the methodical logician of Romans or Galatians. He was that, for his books do manifest a logical, argumentative style of writing. This epistle, however, is emotional, full of tears and grief. It was written more with the heart than with the head. With the exception of Philemon, it is the most personal and the least doctrinal of Paul's epistles. Greek students can testify to the change of writing style and vocabulary as they move from the first to the second letter in translation work. Second Corinthians is difficult to translate because Paul could hardly wait to get the words written to express the burden of his heart to the church.

This book carefully examines the character and the tactics of the false teachers that Paul encountered wherever he went. They were Jews (11:22), claiming to be the ministers of Christ (11:23). Paul, however, saw them differently; he characterized them as false apostles, as deceitful workers, and as Satan's ministers of righteousness

(11:13–15). They apparently carried letters of commendation as their credentials to be given opportunities of public ministry and be provided with financial support (3:1). They viciously criticized Paul's physical appearance, poor oratory (10:10; 11:6), and his refusal to accept money for spiritual service (11:7–12). And they questioned the authenticity of his apostleship (11:5; 12:11–12). Paul saw them as proponents of "another" faith and thus subject to the divine anathema: "For if he that cometh preacheth another Jesus, whom we have not preached, or if ye receive another spirit, which ye have not received, or another gospel, which ye have not accepted, ye might well bear with him" (11:4; cf. Gal. 1:6–9).

The person and ministry of Satan are also emphasized in this epistle. Paul identified him as Satan (2:11), the god of this world (4:4), the serpent (11:3), and as an angel of light (11:14). In relation to Christians, Satan tries to keep them from forgiving one another (2:10–11), attempts to deceive and to corrupt their minds (11:3), and is permitted by God to afflict them physically for their own spiritual protection (12:7–9). In relation to the unsaved, he blinds their minds so that they reject the gospel message (4:4) and promotes a philosophy of human self-righteousness to keep men from accepting the divine righteousness of Christ (11:15).

1

The Necessity of Sufferings

II Corinthians 1:1-14

How would you react if someone you loved hurt you with malicious gossip? What would you do if someone turned the loyalty and affection of your children away from you? This was like Paul's dilemma. False teachers had infiltrated the Corinthian assembly and had questioned both his personal integrity and apostolic authority. Paul expected that such attacks would be made (cf. Acts 20:28–31; Rom. 16:17–18), but he did not expect that the Corinthians would actually believe these erroneous reports. His spiritual children no longer obeyed and loved him as they once did (cf. I Cor. 4:14–15; II Cor. 12:15). Paul was crushed and heartbroken. What could he do about this desperate situation? But he did act!

First of all, he made a trip across the Aegean Sea to Corinth, but that ended in disappointment (2:1). He then sent a letter expressing his deep sorrow and loving concern over their spiritual condition (2:4). Titus, the letter carrier, was commissioned by Paul to seek the reconciliation of the disobedient Corinthians. Finally, these efforts bore fruit. Titus returned to Paul with news that a revival had broken out, that the church was sorry for its sin, and that they wanted to see Paul. Pockets of resistance, however, still remained. Paul felt it was necessary to write again.

In this letter, he defended himself against the remaining accusations: Why did he have so much hardship in the discharge of his ministry? Why did he change his travel plans? Why was his ministry so different from that of the false teachers? Why was he collecting money? Why did he keep silent about his personal achievements for the Lord?

I. SALUTATION (1:1–2)

In his opening remarks, the apostle included what is normally found in his greetings: identification of self, associate, and readers, along with introductory blessings. In this case, however, he omitted a prayer of thanksgiving (cf. Rom. 1:8; Phil. 1:3; Col. 1:3; I Thess. 1:2; II Thess. 1:3). Even the first epistle, written to correct many personal, moral, and doctrinal problems, contained an opening prayer of thanksgiving (cf. I Cor. 1:4–9). Actually, the salutation is shorter than the one in the stern letter to the Galatians (cf. Gal. 1:1–5). Perhaps, Paul wanted to move quickly to the defense of his hardships for which he praised God (1:3; cf. Eph. 1:3).

A. Author (1:1a)

1. His name

In his pre-Christian life, Paul was known as Saul of Tarsus, the persecutor of the church (Acts 7:58; 8:1, 3; 9:1). When Christ revealed Himself to the young Pharisee, He addressed the latter as Saul (Acts 9:4). For the next nine years of his Christian life, he maintained the usage of his given name (Acts 9:17, 19, 22, 26; 11:25, 30; 13:1–2).

At the beginning of his missionary journey, however, he changed his name to Paul (cf. Acts 13:9, 13). On this occasion, at Cyprus, Paul demonstrated his apostolic authority for the first time by imposing blindness upon the

A corner of the Roman forum in Salamis. The forum existed in the times of Barnabas and Paul.

sorcerer Elymas, who had resisted the gospel witness. Through this miracle, Paul won his first convert, the Roman proconsul Sergius Paulus (Acts 13:7–12). It is plausible that Saul assumed the name of Paul *(Paulos)* as a constant reminder of the grace and power of God, who can save sinners and call them to Christian service.[1]

The Latin *paulus* means "little" or "small." Before God, Paul saw himself in this fashion: "Unto me, who am less than the least of all saints, is this grace given, that I should preach among the Gentiles the unsearchable riches of Christ" (Eph. 3:8). Late in life, the apostle still viewed himself as the "chief" of sinners (I Tim. 1:15).

Born into the Jewish tribe of Benjamin, he was probably named by his parents after the name of the first king of Israel (Phil. 3:5; cf. I Sam. 9:1–2). King Saul, who was tall

1. Two early church fathers, Jerome and Augustine, both believed that Paul took his new name from Sergius Paulus.

physically, was humbled by God because of his pride and arrogant self-will. The proud Pharisee was also humbled by God on the road to Damascus, but he arose to become a dedicated servant of Christ.

Paul's own name personified those qualities that the false teachers despised and attacked. They were proud and self-assertive; thus, they criticized Paul for his meek behavior (cf. 10:10).

2. His position

Paul immediately claimed his authority. *First,* he asserted that he was "an apostle."[2] Apostles were those believers who had seen the resurrected Christ and who had been commissioned directly by Him to preach and to lay the foundation for the church age (Eph. 2:20). Their ministries were marked by miraculous authentication and by the obedience of genuine, spiritual Christians. Throughout the Corinthian correspondence, this ring of authority can be detected in Paul's words (I Cor. 1:17; 2:13; 3:10; 4:9, 18–21; 5:4; 7:10; 9:1–6; 11:1; 12:28; 15:8–10; II Cor. 1:1; 12:12).

Second, he stated that he was an apostle "of Jesus Christ." He was not personally appointed by either Ananias or Barnabas (Acts 9:10–18, 27; 11:25–26), nor was he voted into that office by the other apostles, as was

2. The Greek word *apostolos,* translated "apostle," comes from the verb *apostellō*, which means to send away with a commission to do something. The original twelve apostles were selected from among many disciples to be with Christ and to be sent forth by Him to preach, heal, and cast out demons within Israel (Matt. 10:5–8; Mark 3:13–15). Excluding Judas Iscariot, the group was later recommissioned by the resurrected Christ to preach the gospel throughout the world (Matt. 28:16–20).

Matthias (Acts 1:15–26). Rather, he saw Christ in a post-ascension appearance and was directly called by Him (Acts 26:12–20; Gal. 1:1, 11–16). His critics, on the other hand, were "false apostles," men who had transformed "themselves into the apostles of Christ" (11:13). The apostates charged that Paul did not look or act like a real apostle (10:10). Paul affirmed that although his critics looked like apostles, actually they were false. God looks on the heart, not at outward appearance.

Third, the agency of his apostleship was "by the will of God." It was God the Father who decreed both Paul's salvation and apostleship.

B. Associate (1:1b)

The Corinthian church knew Timothy well.[3] He labored with Paul and Silas in the initial evangelization of the city during the apostle's second missionary journey (Acts 18:5). From Ephesus, during the third journey, Paul sent his young associate to Corinth to remind the believers of the apostle's teaching (I Cor. 4:17). Now, Paul included Timothy as a co-defender of the apostle's position and practice. Timothy doubtless furnished some of the information about the spiritual condition of the church (cf. I Cor. 16:10–11).

Paul usually identified Timothy as his son in the faith (I Cor. 4:17; I Tim. 1:2; II Tim. 1:2), but here he is seen as "our brother." Since Paul had led Timothy and many of the Corinthians to saving faith in Christ, he wanted the Corinthians to have the same respect for him as Timothy did.

3. His name means "one who honors God" or "one whom God honors."

C. Readers (1:1c)

1. The church

Paul still regarded his readers as "the church of God" in spite of their problems. They were members of the one true church that Christ built and purchased through His redemptive death and resurrection (Matt. 16:18; Acts 20:28; Eph. 5:25). The church has, as the mystical body of Christ, an organic unity that cannot be divided by imperfect members (John 17:21; I Cor. 12:12–13; Eph. 4:4–6).[4]

In addition to this spiritual identification, the Corinthian believers had a specific earthly location. They comprised the local church "at Corinth." Earlier, the apostle had said to them: "Now ye are the body of Christ, and members in particular" (I Cor. 12:27). They were *the* church *in* Corinth, but they were only a part of the entire true church.

2. The saints

This letter was also addressed to those believers who resided in the Roman province of "Achaia" (the entire area south of Macedonia in the Greek peninsula) but who were not members of the local church at Corinth. This would include Christians at Athens (Acts 17:34) and the local church at Cenchrea (Rom. 16:1–2).

4. The Greek word for "church" *(ekklēsia)* is used in four different ways: (1) It referred to a secular assembly gathered together for civil business (Acts 19:32, 39, 41). (2) Stephen equated Israel in her wilderness wanderings with a church (Acts 7:38). (3) The local church was a group of believers meeting in a specific locality (Rom. 16:5). (4) The universal church includes all believers from the descent of the Holy Spirit on the Day of Pentecost to the return of Christ for His own.

These believers are called "saints." A saint is a sinner saved by the grace of God.[5] He has called upon Christ for salvation and has forever been set apart to God out from a condemned world. This title is a positional name for each child of God (Rom. 1:7; I Cor. 1:2; Eph. 1:1; Phil. 1:1; Col. 1:2).

D. Blessing (1:2)

The content of the blessing was twofold: "grace" and "peace." These two words reflect both Greek ("grace," *charis*) and Hebrew ("peace," *shalom*) concepts. Grace precedes, and is always the basis for, peace. The doctrine of grace reveals that God bestows blessings upon believers apart from any merit within them.

The source of double blessing is from two persons within the divine Being: the "Father" and the Son, the "Lord Jesus Christ."[6] One preposition, "from" *(apo),* links the Father and the Son together as the common source. Doubtless, these blessings are mediated to the child of God through the indwelling ministry of the Holy Spirit.

In spite of the grief and heartache that the church thrust upon the apostle, he wanted them to experience God's sustaining grace and peace.

5. The word "saints" *(hagiois)* means "set apart ones." It is based upon the verb "to sanctify" *(hagiazō),* which is used to describe four different stages in the believer's salvation. It refers to the ministry of the Holy Spirit in the person's life before conversion (Gal. 1:15; II Thess. 2:13); the time of regeneration (I Cor. 6:11; Heb. 10:14); the present cleansing ministry by the Spirit through the Word of God (John 17:17); and the total separation from the effects of sin when the believer receives the incorruptible, immortal body (Eph. 5:26–27).

6. The deity of Jesus Christ is affirmed in this verse by the divine title "Lord" (I Cor. 8:6; Phil. 2:11) and by His union with the Father as a common source of blessing.

II. LESSONS OF SUFFERINGS (1:3–11)

Paul was not ashamed of his sufferings; rather, he gloried in them (cf. 12:9–11). He did not view his hardships as something inconsistent with his apostolic office. He cited them as part of his defense against the false charges levied at him (cf. Gal. 6:11–13). Concerning his critics, he asserted: "From henceforth let no man trouble me: for I bear in my body the marks of the Lord Jesus" (Gal. 6:17). To Paul, the difficulties in his life were essential for learning valuable lessons from God, which he could use in his own ministry and share with others.

A. From God (1:3–5)

1. Character of God (1:3)

Through his sufferings Paul learned three things about the character of God that he could not learn from others or from a textbook. *First,* God is "blessed." All believers are quick to acknowledge the blessedness of God when they have been blessed "with all spiritual blessings in heavenly places in Christ" (Eph. 1:3). It takes a tender, yielded spirit, however, to confess with Job: ". . . the Lord gave, and the Lord hath taken away; blessed be the name of the Lord" (Job 1:21). The patriarch said that after all of his wealth and children had been taken away from him through divine permission.

Second, He is the "Father of mercies." The word for "mercies" *(oiktirmōn)* always appears in the plural, showing the availability of all types of mercies for different kinds of difficulties (cf. Rom. 12:1; Phil. 2:1; Col. 3:12; Heb. 10:28). Here Paul's description of God reflects David's confidence: "Like as a father pitieth his children, so the Lord pitieth them that fear him" (Ps. 103:13).

Third, He is "the God of all comfort." God is not sadistic or capricious; He does not delight in the hard times that come to His children. He is the source of good and perfect gifts (James 1:17). He is not indifferent to the cries of help that come from His own. Rather, He understands and draws near to encourage and strengthen the Christian.[7] All three persons of the Trinity administer comfort to the believer: the Father (1:3–4), the Son (John 14:16, 18; Heb. 2:18; I John 2:1), and the Holy Spirit (John 14:16–17, 26).

2. *Comfort of God (1:4)*

Paul learned that the only source of genuine comfort was the God of comfort. This comfort was personal ("us") and applicable in all situations ("in all our tribulation"). The apostle counted on God to see him through each difficulty. As Jesus promised all believers: "In the world ye shall have tribulation: but be of good cheer; I have overcome the world" (John 16:33). When a person experiences various types of trials he learns more about the comfort of God.

Also, after a believer has experienced different kinds of tribulation, then he better understands the sufferings of others.[8] If he has been comforted by God, then he can comfort others by sharing with them how he was comforted in a similar situation. Paul recognized that as God had led him through various hardships he developed maximum effectiveness in dealing with needy people. Both James and Peter asserted that trials are designed by God to strengthen believers (James 1:2–12; I Peter 1:7). For faith-

7. According to the Greek, a comforter *(paraklētos)* is one who is called beside the needy to help him. The Greek word, either in a noun or verb form, appears ten times in this section (1:3–7).

8. Both "tribulation" and "trouble" come from the same Greek word *thlipsis.*

ful Christians, trials should not be evaluated as chastisement for sin or as a withdrawal of divine blessing.

3. Identification with Christ (1:5)

Paul learned that the real essence of the spiritual life was in genuine identification with Christ in His sacrificial, redemptive work (Phil. 1:21). His goal was to know "the fellowship of [Christ's] sufferings, being made conformable unto his death" (Phil. 3:10).

He learned that comfort comes only through suffering. And, he found out that the comfort is greater than the hardship.

Not all suffering, however, results in divine comfort. Only specific suffering qualifies. When "the sufferings of Christ" abound in a believer, then he can experience the abundant consolation that comes from Christ. Peter commented: "For what glory is it, when ye be buffeted for your faults, ye shall take it patiently? but if, when ye do well, and suffer for it, ye take it patiently, this is acceptable with God" (I Peter 2:20).

Just as Christ suffered for him, Paul was willing to suffer for Christ. Just as Christ had to suffer to gain glory, so Paul knew that his suffering would gain consolation.[9]

B. For Others (1:6–7)

1. Example for others (1:6)

Paul was aware that God was working through his experiences of affliction and comfort to make of him an example or a pattern for others to follow. On another occasion, he confessed: ". . . that in me first Jesus Christ might show forth all long suffering, for a pattern to them

9. The words "comfort" and "consolation" come from the same Greek word *paraklēsis*.

which should hereafter believe on him to life everlasting" (I Tim. 1:16). The apostle knew that if God could save him, a blasphemous persecutor, then God could save anyone. A believer could look at Paul and conclude that if God could comfort and deliver the apostle from his *many* afflictions, He could also comfort another Christian through lesser hardships. Few have suffered more for their faith than Paul; few have experienced more difficulties than this great apostle.

The double usage of "whether" shows the two purposes of his example: the first in affliction and the second in comfort. Both are to result in the believer's "consolation and salvation." The Christian should expect to experience hardships, and he should also "endure" them in the same way that the apostle did. In this way, encouragement by example can pass from one generation to another. Paul commended the Thessalonians in this area: "And ye became followers of us, and of the Lord, having received the word in much affliction, with joy of the Holy Ghost: So that ye were ensamples to all that believe in Macedonia and Achaia" (I Thess. 1:6–7).

2. *Confidence in others (1:7)*

Paul believed that what God had done for him He would do for others. He had a stedfast "hope," a firm conviction that the Corinthians would have victory through their sufferings. He knew that they would be "partakers" of suffering in the will of God along with Christ and Paul.[10] With equal confidence, he knew that they would also share in the "consolation." Biblical consolation involves more than just feeling sorry for someone who is in difficulty; it

10. The word "partakers" is based upon the Greek *koinōnoi,* which conveys the ideas of sharing and fellowship.

connotes active encouragement and help to see the person through his trouble. God never promised to keep us out of the furnace of trials. Rather, He has pledged to be with us in the fire and to lead us out of the oppressive flames. Elsewhere, Paul wrote for our encouragement: "Being confident of this very thing, that he which hath begun a good work in you will perform it until the day of Jesus Christ" (Phil. 1:6). No believer is alone in hard times; God is there beside him.

C. For Self (1:8–11)

1. Rejection of self (1:8–9a)

Paul did not trust in his own wisdom or physical strength to endure trials. He urged his readers to learn the same lesson through referring to the "trouble" that came to him in the Roman province of Asia, where Ephesus was located. The Corinthians were aware of Paul's persecutions, but they did not realize their full intensity and Paul's reaction to them. This trouble might have been a severe illness or the peril of martyrdom, most probably the latter. In the first epistle, he mentioned that he had "fought with beasts at Ephesus" and that he had "many adversaries" to his preaching (I Cor. 15:32; 16:9). Although he was prevented by friends from entering the amphitheater, where his companions Gaius and Aristarchus had been forcefully taken by the enraged pagans, that incident prompted the apostle to leave Ephesus (Acts 19:29–31; 20:1). He later remarked that Aquila and Priscilla had "laid down their own necks" for him (Rom. 16:3–4).

Paul described the intensity of his trouble in three ways. *First,* he was "pressed out of measure, above strength."[11]

11. The Greek literally reads "according to extreme excess we were weighted down beyond ability."

Like a beast of burden he was crushed beneath a load too heavy to bear. Physically and psychologically, he could not humanly cope with the situation. *Second,* he fully expected to be martyred in the midst of his trouble. Without God's help he saw no way out of his predicament. *Third,* he had "the sentence of death" in himself. The word "sentence" *(apokrima)* is based upon the verb "to answer" *(apokrinomai).* Often, it referred to a judicial sentence or to an official decision based upon a legal inquiry. This may mean that a pagan or Jewish group had made an official attempt to effect Paul's execution.[12] Jewish leaders under Caiaphas made a similar type of decision to bring about the crucifixion of Christ (John 11:53). Later, when Paul was under Roman custody in Jerusalem, a band of over forty conspired to kill the apostle (Acts 23:12–13).

Paul affirmed that the divine purpose behind such a trial was "that we should not trust in ourselves."[13] When a believer realizes that he can no longer control his circumstances, then he is willing to yield himself completely to the sovereign, all-inclusive purpose of God.

2. *Trust in God (1:9b–10)*

If any man thought that he alone could solve his problems and then discovered that he could not do it, he would be overwhelmed with total despair. That is why such a man needs to hear the good news of divine deliverance. From his precarious situation, Paul learned that he could

12. The perfect tense "had" *(eschēkamen)* indicates that the sentence was still in effect even though Paul had left Ephesus for Macedonia.

13. The words "should not trust" come from the Greek *mē pepoithotes ōmen,* which involves the usage of the perfect participle in a periphrastic construction with the present subjunctive of "to be." This means that Paul had a crisis experience in which he learned a lesson that continued to dominate his pattern of life.

put his trust in God, who would support and deliver him at all times, in all places, and under all circumstances.[14]

To describe God's power, Paul identified Him as the one who "raiseth the dead." The two greatest prospects that man faces in this life are spiritual death and physical death. If God can quicken a dead sinner and give him spiritual life, then He can solve man's present spiritual, mental, and emotional needs. If God can raise the physical dead and give him an immortal, incorruptible, and resurrection body, He then can deliver man from his present physical problems.

God is the same, yesterday, today, and forever. He does not change. Thus, Paul knew that as God had rescued him from *past* threats to his life, He would preserve him through his *present* experiences, and that He could also deliver him from any *future* assassination plot. God watches His own; therefore believers can have assurance that nothing in the present or future "shall be able to separate [them] from the love of God, which is in Christ Jesus [their] Lord" (Rom. 8:38–39).

3. Help from others (1:11)

Paul also felt sustained by others during his sufferings. It is sometimes hard for a believer to admit that he needs the help of others. He may feel that such an admission reflects weakness. Many Christians try to impress others with their self-sufficiency; thus cries for help are rarely and reluctantly expressed. Paul, however, willingly and openly declared his thanks for help given to him during his periods of suffering.

Paul recognized that the Corinthians had helped him in two ways: by their prayers and by their gift. They had

14. The Greek word for "in" is *epi,* normally translated as "upon." Confidence must be built upon God and not upon self.

prayed for the apostle, and God had answered their prayers. Paul often requested prayer in his behalf (Col. 4:3) and he knew that God used the prayers of others to effect his deliverance from prison and similar crises (Phil. 1:19; Philem. v. 22). On the efficacy of intercessory prayer, Hughes observed: "In prayer, human impotence casts itself at the feet of divine omnipotence. Thus, the duty of prayer is not a modification of God's power, but a glorification of it."[15]

In addition, they had helped Paul with their "gift." The gift *(charisma)* may refer to money, which eased a financial need (I Cor. 16:7), or to internal release from anxiety produced by the coming of Titus and his good report of the Corinthian revival (7:5–7).

III. RESULTS OF SUFFERING (1:12–14)

Through hardships and the lessons learned from them, various qualities of Paul's character were manifested. In defense of his personal conduct, the apostle mentioned three of them.

A. Integrity (1:12)

It is not wrong to share what God has done in your life.[16] Silence, in fact, is an unnatural indication of gratefulness.

1. Of character (1:12a)

Paul had a clear conscience. He could testify to the truthfulness of the claims that he was going to make about

15. Philip Edgcumbe Hughes, *Paul's Second Epistle to the Corinthians,* New International Commentary on the New Testament (Grand Rapids: Wm. B. Eerdmans Publishing Co., 1962), p. 23.

16. The word "rejoicing" *(kauchēsis)* literally refers to an act of glorying or boasting.

himself. *First,* his life was marked by "simplicity." This word *(aplotēti)* indicates single-minded purpose. Paul lived for the glory of God and for the service of others. *Second,* he manifested "godly sincerity." The word for "sincerity" *(eilikrineia)* literally means "judged by the sun." Ancient jars and vases were examined for disguised cracks by holding them up against the rays of the sun. Paul knew that God could not detect flaws in his spiritual motivation. Men can fool other men, but they cannot fool God. *Third,* he did not employ "fleshly wisdom." Earlier, the apostle condemned the folly of the world's wisdom, which, unfortunately, was expressed by carnal believers (I Cor. 1:17–25; 3:1–4). Rather, Paul thought God's thoughts after Him. He spoke the wisdom of God revealed by the Holy Spirit (I Cor. 2:6–13).

2. Of conduct (1:12b)

Paul knew that he was what he was by "the grace of God" and that he did what he did by that same divine grace (I Cor. 15:10). This truth will result in a sameness of conduct. The apostle did not act one way "in the world" and in an altogether different fashion before the churches ("to you-ward"). He lived above reproach in both realms. He unashamedly could confess: "Ye are witnesses, and God also, how holily and justly and unblameably we behaved ourselves among you that believe" (I Thess. 2:10).

B. Consistency (1:13)

The apostle claimed that what he wrote about himself was what they should expect to read about him. His critics asserted that Paul wrote one thing and meant something else by it. They charged that Paul's expression in writing and in actual behavior did not match (10:9–10). The apostle denied the presence of innuendos or reservations within his writings. He wrote only what his readers could understand clearly. They did not have to "read between the lines" to get his true meaning.

The usage of the two verbs "read" *(anaginōskō)* and "acknowledge" *(epiginōskō)* refer to written and oral testimony respectively. What they both read and heard from Paul were consistent. What they read from Paul and what they heard from Titus or Timothy about Paul also matched.

Many in the Corinthian church had already acknowledged Paul to be consistent when he was present or absent, when he was preaching or writing, and when he was suffering or comforting others. It was Paul's hope that this conviction would continue into the future until the end of his life or the coming of Christ (I Cor. 1:8).[17]

C. Mutual Rejoicing (1:14)

Paul recognized that their understanding of his behavior and motivation was only partial ("in part"). Usually, human evaluation of spirituality in others is in this fashion (I Cor. 2:15). In spite of this, the majority now rejoiced and boasted about the achievements of the apostle in their midst. When Paul learned of their feelings from Titus, he "rejoiced the more" (7:6–7). He assured the Corinthians that he would boast about them in the future, especially at the coming of Christ ("in the day of the Lord Jesus"). To others, he expressed the same joy: "For what is our hope, or joy, or crown of rejoicing? Are not even ye in the presence of our Lord Jesus Christ at his coming" (I Thess. 2:19)? Their mutual rejoicing over each other in the present would also be manifested in the future.

17. Note the switch from the present to the future tense of "acknowledge."

QUESTIONS FOR DISCUSSION

1. How can a man determine whether he is in the ministry by the will of God, by the will of others, or by his own will? How can a church that is looking for a pastor detect that such a person has really been called by God into the ministry?

2. What kinds of trials should a believer expect to experience in this life? Is he immune from any of the problems that the unsaved encounter?

3. How can believers share their experiences of suffering and comfort with others? Should time be set aside in regular services for such testimonies?

4. Why do believers today have an attitude toward hardships different than Paul's?

5. Are believers afraid to express publicly their inner feelings about themselves? Should this be done? If so, how?

6. How can believers assist other Christians who are enduring difficulty? Do cards and visits suffice?

7. Are today's Christians consistent? Are they the same on Monday as they are on Sunday? What can be done to promote constancy of behavior?

2

The Expressions of Spiritual Concern

II Corinthians 1:15—2:13

In the first section of this epistle, Paul defended his personal conduct, and he discussed why he had to suffer so much for Christ (1:1–14). Now he explains why he changed his travel plans (1:15–2:1) and why he wanted a repentant offender to be forgiven (2:2–13). In so doing, Paul manifests his deep spiritual concern for the Corinthians' Christian growth and for his apostolic relationship to them.

I. IN HIS TRAVEL PLANS (1:15–2:1)

Paul was faithful in his present responsibilities, but he still made plans for the future. Plans should not be made without consulting God, but it is right to project future goals within the will of God (cf. James 4:13–17). This is what Paul did. He planned future missionary trips although he knew that the sovereign God could change his destination and timing. On his second trip, he attempted to evangelize both Asia and Bithynia, but the Holy Spirit prevented him (Acts 16:6–8). He informed the Roman Christians that he planned to visit them on his way to Spain after he had first gone to Jerusalem (Rom. 15:24–25). Paul made travel plans constantly, but when those plans were altered by God, he did not resist the change. Rather, he manifested his submission to the divine will by prompt obedience.

A. The Plans Revealed (1:15–16)

Actually, these plans differed from those he declared in the first epistle (I Cor. 16:5–8). In that passage, he stated that he would remain at Ephesus until Pentecost, that he would then journey to Macedonia and later to Corinth, that he would spend the winter in Corinth, and that he would proceed on to Jerusalem. Therefore, the apostle really had to explain a double change in plans.

1. To minister to them (1:15)

Paul had "confidence" that God would lead him to Corinth again and that his ministry would be accepted.[1] He "was minded" to visit Corinth two more times during his present missionary travels, but his original purpose was not to be realized.[2] Paul was willing to go to Corinth twice, but he did not want to go where he was not welcome.

The "second benefit" does not refer to a post conversion experience in the lives of the believers. It does not point to a second work of grace, which some call the infilling or the baptism in the Holy Spirit. It is explained in the next verse as a double visit by Paul to the church instead of just one, as originally stated in the first epistle.

1. The word for "confidence" *(pepoithēsei)* is built upon the verbal form of "trust" *(pepoithotes;* 1:9).

2. The words "I was minded" are literally translated "I was willing" *(eboulomēn;* cf. II Peter 3:9).

2. To visit them twice (1:16)

To give the Corinthians a double exposure to his ministry, Paul had decided to go directly from Ephesus to Corinth across the Aegean Sea; then north to the Macedonian cities of Philippi, Thessalonica, and Berea; come "again" to Corinth (the "second benefit"); and later sail for Jerusalem from Corinth. His purpose in going to Judea was to take the collection that the Gentile churches were amassing for the needy Christians in Jerusalem. From Jerusalem, Paul then planned to venture west, to Italy (Rome) and Spain. Nearing the end of his earthly ministry, he knew that likely he would never visit Corinth again. This is why he changed his earlier plans to the ones presently mentioned (cf. I Cor. 16:5–7). However, he even changed this second set of plans.

B. The Change Explained (1:17–2:1)

Paul's critics took advantage of this change in plans and sought to discredit him as a vacillating, weak person. They misinterpreted the apostle's actions and misapplied his motivations. Paul thus had to defend his integrity by explaining why he changed his plans twice. In so doing, he revealed certain aspects of his personality.

1. He was not indecisive (1:17–18)

It was easy for the apostle's critics to say that he was fickle. To them, a double change of plans implied an unstable person, one who was trying to manipulate events by himself without consulting the will of God.

Paul countered the charge with a double question, both pertaining to the resolution of his will.[3] *First,* he denied

3. Both the words "minded" and "purpose" come from the same Greek word *boulomai.*

that he did not put much thought into his plans. *Second,* he denied that he made plans based upon a sin-dominated will. His plans were not merely human; rather, his plans were divinely directed. Although his plans were not made out of "lightness" or "according to the flesh," Paul was not adamant in his decision to go somewhere or to do something. He was not so unalterable that his "yea" would always remain as "yea" and his "nay, nay." His mind could be changed at the last moment if he knew that God was leading him in another direction. Just as God willed to destroy Nineveh for its wickedness and later willed not to destroy the city for its repentance, so Paul's purpose changed (cf. Jer. 18:7; Jonah 3:4, 9). In a sense, God's "yea" was changed to a "nay." God certainly is not vacillating in His person (Mal. 3:6; James 1:17). He is immutable, but He is not inflexible. His purposes for men change as men change in their spiritual relationships toward Him.

Paul claimed that he was not a "yes and no man." He did not say yes and mean no, or vice versa. He knew that his yes meant yes and that his no meant no. Thus, his change of plans did not manifest a weakness in his character. He did not violate the admonition of James that echoes the words of Jesus: ". . . swear not, neither by heaven, neither by the earth, neither by any other oath: but let your yea be yea; and your nay, nay; lest ye fall into condemnation" (James 5:12; cf. Matt. 5:37).

2. *He was positive (1:19–22)*

Paul lived by conviction, not by doubt. It is true that "a double minded man is unstable in all his ways" (James 1:8), but Paul was single minded in purpose and action. He stated his positive assurance in three areas.

First, he knew that what he preached about Christ was true (1:19). He knew that their missionary team, Paul, Silas, and Timothy, evangelized Corinth with redemptive truth (cf. Acts 18:1–17). He knew that Jesus Christ was the Son of God, that God had become man, and that Christ had two natures (divine and human) within His single person. Christ's incarnate purpose did not fluctuate. He came to die. Christ Himself said: "Even as the Son of man came not to be ministered unto, but to minister and to give his life a ransom for many" (Matt. 20:28). And yet, prior to His crucifixion, He prayed three times: "O my Father, if it be possible, let this cup pass from me: nevertheless not as I will, but as thou wilt" (Matt. 26:39). This intercession does not imply that Christ was unstable or vacillating. Neither does Paul's change of travel plans imply that he was fickle.

Second, he knew that the "promises of God" were true (1:20). The most sincere person can make a promise and yet be unable to keep it. To keep a promise every time, one must know all of the present and future circumstances and must have the power to control all contingencies. No man can do this, but God can. He is both omniscient and omnipotent. God makes both conditional and unconditional promises. A conditional promise will be fulfilled only if a person obeys the specific will of God (cf. II Chron. 7:14). An unconditional promise will be fulfilled whether or not man is obedient (cf. John 14:3). The apostle claimed that "all the promises of God *in him* [Christ]" are unconditional. Because a believer is *in Christ,* he can have absolute assurance that he will have all that the Father has promised him (cf. Rom. 11:26–29).

These promises have a double guarantee of fulfillment ("Yea" and "Amen"). Both the Father and the Son have pledged their word. Whenever Christ wanted to affirm a theological truth, He began with the words: "Verily, verily" (literally "Amen, Amen," John 3:5). Christ said of Himself: "These things saith the Amen, the faithful and true witness" (Rev. 3:14).

Although believers profit from the fulfillment of divine promises, the ultimate purpose behind them is "the glory of God by us." We glorify God when we recognize Him to be what He really is. When the promises of God come to pass, then believers can fully perceive that God faithfully keeps His word to His own.

Third, he knew that God had worked in his life (1:21–22). The apostle specifically mentioned four areas.

(1) God was presently "establishing" Paul.[4] This verb is normally translated as "confirms" *(bebaiōn;* cf. I Cor. 1:6). This verb is used in the early Greek papyri for the legal sense of guarantee. Thus, God was guaranteeing or authenticating Paul's ministry to be true and authoritative by giving sign gifts through the apostle.[5] The Corinthians ("with you") should have readily recognized this when Paul originally evangelized them "in demonstration of the Spirit and of power" (I Cor. 2:4). Christ "confirmed the word of the apostles by the signs that followed" (Mark 16:20). The Book of Hebrews adds that what was spoken by the Lord "was confirmed unto us by them that heard him; God also bearing them witness both with signs and

4. This verb is a present participle, whereas the next three are aorist participles. This shows that God had done three things once and for all in his life, whereas the confirmation was constant.

5. Cf. J. Lanier Burns, "A Reemphasis on the Purpose of the Sign Gifts," *Bibliotheca Sacra* (July-September, 1975). Burns gives a convincing argument to show that the verb "confirm" refers to a divine authentication of authoritative, inspired revelation, whether oral or written. This confirmation thus was withdrawn when new revelation ceased at the end of the canon.

wonders, and with divers miracles, and gifts of the Holy Ghost, according to his own will" (2:3–4).

(2) God had "anointed" Paul. All genuine believers have been anointed by God (cf. I John 2:20). This occurs at the moment of regeneration, when the repentant sinner is initially filled and permanently indwelt with the Holy Spirit. Just as the divine-human Christ did not begin His public ministry of preaching until He was anointed with the Spirit at His baptism (Luke 3:21–22; 4:17–21), so no person can do anything for God unless the Holy Spirit is within him.

(3) God had "sealed" Paul. All believers are sealed with the "Holy Spirit of promise" at the time of conversion (Eph. 1:13). This sealing ministry is permanent "until the day of redemption" (Eph. 4:30). Chronologically, it occurs when a sinner believes; logically, it occurs after he believes.[6] The Spirit Himself is the seal; God seals us with none other than Himself. Elsewhere, Paul wrote: "Nevertheless the foundation of God standeth sure, having this seal, the Lord knoweth them that are his" (II Tim. 2:19). God knows who His children are by the indwelling presence of the Holy Spirit, who bears witness with the human spirit as to their spiritual identity (Rom. 8:16). Daniel was placed in a lions' den that was sealed with the king's signet to prevent the stone from being removed from the entrance (Dan. 6:17). The tomb of Christ was sealed as a guarantee of official security. The seal thus was a sign of ownership and protection.

(4) God had "given the earnest of the Spirit" to Paul (cf. 5:5). The term "earnest" *(arrabōn)* refers to a down payment to secure a purchase. It was a guarantee that the buyer would eventually pay the total purchase price. It

6. For example, the wedding kiss occurs when the couple is married, but logically, it happens after they have been legally joined.

also referred in ancient culture to a gift that a man would give to a woman as an expression of his love for her and of his desire to marry her. It would correspond to the modern engagement ring. Again, the Holy Spirit Himself is "the earnest." Paul wrote that He "is the earnest of our inheritance until the redemption of the purchased possession" (Eph. 1:14). Although the believer has already been blessed with bountiful spiritual gifts, he does not yet have all of what has been graciously provided through Christ's redemptive death. These riches will be gained at Christ's return and enjoyed thoroughly in eternity. Believers today only have "the first fruits of the Spirit" (Rom. 8:23); the full harvest of salvation blessings is yet to come, and the Christian can have full assurance that he will receive it.

Just as Christ pledged the fulfillment of His word through the indwelling earnest of the Spirit, so Paul had pledged his word that he would return to Corinth (I Cor. 16:5). Although he had changed his travel plans twice, he had not removed his guarantee to return. Paul wanted the church to know that they could count on his word, just as believers can trust the promises of Christ.

3. He was sensitive (1:23–2:1)

Paul was unafraid to face the Corinthians, contrary to what his critics charged. They claimed that the apostle changed his plans twice and that he sent Titus out of fear that his personal authority would be rejected. Appealing to God as his witness, Paul defended his integrity ("Moreover I call God for a record upon my soul"). He often did this (Rom. 1:9; Gal. 1:20; Phil. 1:8; I Thess. 2:5, 10). He believed that God knew what his inner feelings were when he changed his travel plans. Now, he wanted his Corinthian readers to know three reasons why he delayed his visit.

First, he wanted "to spare" them (1:23b). In the first epistle, he wrote:

> Now some are puffed up, as though I would not come to you.
>
> But I will come to you shortly, if the Lord will, and will know, not the speech of them which are puffed up, but the power.
>
> For the kingdom of God is not in word, but in power.
>
> What will ye? shall I come unto you with a rod, or in love, and in the spirit of meekness? (I Cor. 4:18–21).

The arrogant minority who opposed Paul were like rebellious children who thought that their father was too weak and afraid to discipline them. As their spiritual father, Paul knew that he had to deal with their disobedience. But he did not want to exercise his apostolic authority if there was no need. He wanted to come as a loving father to children, not as a stern disciplinarian. He wanted to come with his arms outstretched toward them, not with a rod of chastisement in his right hand. To believers under authority, the Book of Hebrews states, "Obey them that have the rule over you, and submit yourselves: for they watch for your souls, as they that must give account, *that they may do it with joy, and not with grief: for that is unprofitable for you*" (Heb. 13:17). As a parent does not enjoy spanking his children, neither did Paul want to go to Corinth to punish his spiritual children.

Second, Paul wished to help them in their spiritual growth (1:24). The genuine Christian experience is a life of faith. Repentant sinners are justified by faith and thereafter should walk by faith. The walk of faith, however, cannot be forced upon unwilling subjects; it must issue voluntarily. Although Paul had authority over them, he did not want them to comply to his dictates superficially. He did not feel that the situation had deteriorated to the point where such extreme pressure by him was needed.

This was his normal procedure in dealing with personal problems. When he wrote Philemon about the proper way to receive the runaway slave Onesimus, who was then converted, the apostle said: "Wherefore, though I might be much bold in Christ to enjoin thee that which is convenient, yet for love's sake I rather beseech thee" (Philem. vv. 8–9). Sensitive spiritual pastors should not be "lords over God's heritage, but [be] ensamples [examples] to the flock" (I Peter 5:3). Jesus Himself cautioned future leaders: "Ye know that the princes of the Gentiles exercise dominion over them, and they that are great exercise authority upon them. But it shall not be so among you: but whosoever will be great among you, let him be your minister" (Matt. 20:25–26). In his next visit to them, Paul wanted their relationship to be marked by joy, mutual labor ("helpers," *sunergoi*), and faith.

Third, he did not want to come "in heaviness" (2:1). The word for "heaviness" *(lupē)* literally means "grief" or "sorrow." He did not want to come with a heavy or broken heart, nor did he want them to have heavy hearts when he arrived.[7] To prevent this situation, he desired to allow God more time in which to produce a revival in the hearts of the Corinthians.

The usage of the adverb "again" has created an interesting question: Did Paul make a quick trip across the Aegean Sea to Corinth between his original evangelization of the city and the writing of this letter, a trip not mentioned in the Book of Acts? If so, it must have ended in disappointment. That is why Paul did not want to make another trip in heaviness of heart. Later, he does refer to his next trip as the "third time" (12:14; 13:1). Or, the adverbial usage

7. In this passage, three parties are involved in sorrow *(lupē):* the church (2:2), the offender (2:7), and Paul (2:4).

of "again" may mean that Paul wanted his second visit to be like his first visit, which resulted in joy. In that instance, the reference to a third time must be contrasted with an unfulfilled second trip, planned but not carried out. Although no one can be dogmatic, the first view seems to be more plausible.

Paul thus adequately explained why he changed his travel plans. He did it basically for their spiritual benefit, not for his own protection.

II. IN HIS FORGIVENESS (2:2–13)

Solomon wisely observed: "To everything there is a season, and a time to every purpose under the heaven" (Eccles. 3:1). In his famous list (Eccles. 3:2–8), he omitted a contrast that Paul now wanted to emphasize: A time to discipline and a time to forgive. In this section, Paul continued to express his spiritual concern over interpersonal relationships and the essence of forgiveness.

A. Letter of Correction (2:2–4)

Paul, in this section, mentioned the writing of a letter three times (2:3, 4, 9). But which letter is it? There are three possibilities. *First,* it could refer to the first epistle. The offender then could easily be the disciplined fornicator (I Cor. 5). *Second,* it could refer to a lost letter, written after I Corinthians and his unrecorded, disappointing visit and carried to the church by Titus. The offender then could be the leader of an anti-Paul group. *Third,* it could refer to II Corinthians.[8] The offender then could still be a critic of Paul. If the first or second view is cor-

8. The verbs would then be seen as epistolary aorists. The letter thus was present at the time of writing but would be past at its reading.

rect, then the offender had already repented before Paul wrote the second epistle. If the third view is right, then the apostle anticipated that the offender would repent before the arrival of the missionary team. Of the three views, the first two are most probable, the second of which being more plausible.

Regardless, Paul wrote the letter out of concern to manifest two purposes.

1. To produce joy (2:2–3)

Paul realized that he would have to grieve the entire congregation (plural "you," *humas*) to produce grief and brokenness within the key opponent in the church (singular "who is he" and "the same"). He took that risk, and God made it work. Now the apostle wanted them to know that the very same person who was "made sorry" by him had made him "glad." Men view this as a strange twist of fortune, but Paul recognized it as a spiritual paradox under the sovereign control of a gracious God. Grief was turned into joy because the offender repented and was reconciled to both God and Paul.

Paul claimed that he had to write such a painful letter because he did not want to "have sorrow from them of whom [he] ought to rejoice" (2:3a). Here, he moved his attention from the offender (singular) to the group who assisted or tolerated him (plural "them"). He wanted his next visit to be full of joy.

He expected that his feelings were the same as those of the majority within the church (2:3b). He believed that what would make him happy would also give them joy. He wanted to rejoice over all of them, and he desired that all of them would rejoice over him.

2. To demonstrate love (2:4)

The critics admitted that Paul's letters were "weighty and powerful," but they charged that the apostle wanted to "terrify" those who dared to oppose him (10:9–10). He categorically denied that allegation.

Rather, the attitude behind his writing was "out of much affliction and anguish of heart." The usage of the two words of emotion plus the adjective "much" reveal that the apostle was not cold and heartless. Rather, the source ("out of," *ek*) of the epistle was a compassionate, loving concern. In the midst of the outward tribulation produced by the opposing Ephesians, the apostle had an inward "affliction" caused by the unrepentant Corinthians.[9] He was being pressed together both by friends and

9. Both "affliction" (2:4) and "tribulation" (1:4) come from the same Greek word *thlipsis*.

The theatre at Ephesus. This is the scene of the riot during Paul's ministry there. The seating capacity of the theatre is 25,000.

foes, both by the saved and the unsaved, and both inwardly and outwardly. In the New Testament, the word "anguish" *(sunochē)* is used elsewhere only once—of the "distress" that nations will experience in the Day of the Lord when God will give alarming signs in the heavens and on the earth (Luke 21:25).

Paul expressed his inward emotion outwardly "with many tears." As he dictated the letter, he shed and wiped away the tears.[10] This epistle was not a logical treatise (cf. Romans), but, rather, an emotional plea. As Jesus wept over the unbelief of loved ones (Luke 19:41), so the apostle wept often. He warned the Ephesian church about false teachers "night and day with tears" (Acts 20:31) and informed the Philippian church in the same way (Phil. 3:18). He characterized his life as "serving the Lord with all humility of mind, with many tears, and temptations" (Acts 20:19).

He expressed his purpose in writing both negatively and positively (note the double usage of "that," *hina*). He did not want to burden them with grief; rather he wanted them to know how much he loved them.[11]

B. Forgiveness of the Offender (2:5–11)

In the painful letter, Paul outlined the procedure of discipline, which the church obeyed (cf. 2:9). Now, the apostle had to describe the rationale behind the process of reconciliation. Unfortunately, most believers, then and now, know more about the separation of fellowship than they do about its restoration.

10. Possibly because of poor eyesight, Paul usually dictated his letters to an amanuensis. Writing and dictating must be viewed as synonymous.

11. The word "love" is very emphatic, actually occurring before the purpose clause with which it is grammatically connected.

1. His sin (2:5)

Paul felt that the offender had grieved the church more than he had the apostle.[12] Their grief extended beyond discipline and forgiveness; they still were upset over what had happened. On the other hand, Paul admitted that he had been grieved but that he had gotten over it. At this time, he did not want to describe his grief lest he add a further burden of memory upon them ("that I may not overcharge you all"). Paul wisely thought it was not good to resurrect the past performance of forgiven sins lest people go through the inner agony of remorse over them once more.

2. His punishment (2:6)

The church responded to Paul's directives set forth in his letter and through his representative, Titus. They disciplined the offender. If he was the infamous fornicator, he was excommunicated (I Cor. 5:5, 13). If he was a critic of the apostle, then he was also publicly rebuked and/or severed from ecclesiastical fellowship (cf. I Tim. 5:19–20).

Paul believed that the offender had been adequately disciplined by the church. The usage of the adjective "sufficient" suggests that some might have wanted to impose a more severe punishment. Apparently, there was not unanimous support for the action. Only the majority is indicated in the phrase "of many." To Paul, the goal of the painful letter had been reached; now, it was up to the church to proceed to the next level of spiritual brotherhood.

12. The protasis introduced by "if" is based upon the Greek *ei* with the perfect active indicative *lelupēken.* Literally, it reads: "If someone has caused others to be grieved today because of a past action, *and he has.*"

3. His restoration (2:7–11)

The word "contrariwise" shows that Paul wanted the church to change in its attitude and action toward the repentant offender. He outlined five concepts for their guidance in the procedure of reconciliation.

First, they were to prevent the man from drowning in his own grief over what he had done (2:7). Sometimes, even though believers have been forgiven by both God and others, they cannot forgive themselves. They remain embarrassed and develop guilt feelings that can destroy their mental and emotional health. Paul did not want this to take place. He advised the church to assure the repentant offender of their forgiveness and comfort. He wanted the person to know that his past sin would not be held against him.

Second, they were to "confirm [their] love toward him" (2:8). A human covenant, "if it be confirmed," cannot be disannulled or added to (Gal. 3:15). Thus, Paul wanted the church to make an official decision to reconcile the offender, to ratify the resolution by public announcement to all of the members, and to inform the person of the church's action. Genuine love covers a multitude of sins; it "thinketh no evil" (I Cor. 13:5). Paul wanted the offender to know that the church family loved him and wanted him back in their midst.

Third, they were to "be obedient in all things" (2:9). As they submitted themselves to the authority of Paul to discipline the offender, so the apostle wanted them to obey him through forgiving the offender. He saw their reaction to this latest request as "the proof" of their love for him. Christ stated that obedience was the outward demonstration of real inner love (John 14:15). By manifesting forgiving love toward the offender, the church would demonstrate their love for Paul.

Fourth, they were to manifest divine forgiveness in their human forgiveness (2:10). Elsewhere, Paul wrote:

> Put on therefore, as the elect of God, holy and beloved, bowels of mercies, kindness, humbleness of mind, meekness, longsuffering;
> Forbearing one another, and forgiving one another, if any man have a quarrel against any: *even as Christ forgave you, so also do ye.*
> And above all these things put on love, which is the bond of perfectness (Col. 3:12–14).

Their forgiveness was to disclose Paul's forgiveness, which in turn revealed the graciousness of Christ's forgiveness. Forgiveness is part of God's essence; He stands ready to forgive even before He has been asked to forgive. A forgiving spirit does not keep count of the times that a person has sinned against him. Jesus informed Peter that forgiveness goes beyond seven times to "seventy times seven" (Matt. 18:22). If God has forgiven us such a great debt, we should forgive others of comparatively small debts.

Paul's forgiveness of the offender was also for the benefit of the entire church ("for your sakes"). If he could find forgiveness within his heart, then they should be able to do likewise.

He also forgave "in the person of Christ." [13] This could mean that he acted as Christ's authoritative representative. Earlier he had acted with the power of Christ to retain sins (I Cor. 5:5; cf. John 20:23); now he demonstrated his right to remit sins. Or, it could mean that he forgave under Christ's scrutiny. Paul was confident that Christ knew that his forgiveness was actually genuine.

Fifth, they were not to give Satan a spiritual "advantage" (2:11).[14] When Christians do not forgive other

13. Literally "in the face of Christ" or "in the presence of Christ."

14. The word "advantage" is based upon the Greek word normally translated as "covetousness" *(pleoneketō).*

believers, Satan wins a victory. His goal is to destroy personal relationships between God and His children and between Christians.

Believers should recognize Satan as their real enemy. The English word "Satan" is based upon the Hebrew *Satan* and Aramaic *Satana,* which both mean "adversary." They should not be ignorant of "his devices," a word referring to the thoughts and purposes of the mind *(noēma).* Just as Satan filled the heart of Ananias to lie to the Holy Spirit and to the apostles (Acts 5:3), so Satan can fill the mind of the believer with thoughts of bitterness and unforgiving revenge (cf. Eph. 4:31–32).

C. Absence of Titus (2:12–13)

After the uproar in Ephesus, Paul finally left that Asian city after three years of labor. He moved north to the port of Troas where earlier he had received his famous Macedonian vision on his second journey (Acts 16:8–11). Now God opened a door of witness, but Paul felt that he could not remain there. Normally, Paul was thankful for open doors of ministry and entered them (Acts 14:27; I Cor. 16:9; Col. 4:3), but this time he felt differently.

Apparently, Paul had given Titus instructions to rejoin the apostle at Troas, if at all possible. The apostle would have interpreted this brief reunion as a sign of a Corinthian revival. But Titus did not come. The concern of Paul over the safety of Titus, the strained relationship between the church and him, and the reaction to the painful letter intensified. He could not preach as he normally would, so he went on to Macedonia (2:13; cf. Acts 20:1).

Thus, Paul ended this section as he began, by intimately expressing his concern. He wanted the church to know how he really felt about them and how those feelings affected his travel plans and treatment of the offender.

QUESTIONS FOR DISCUSSION

1. What causes people to misinterpret phrases (e.g. "second benefit") by taking them out of their context?

2. How can you determine whether you are making plans according to the will of God or according to the flesh? Can others detect this difference in your life?

3. Why are people so negative about the positive Christian life? What can be done to change this attitude?

4. What is the difference between pastoral authority and leadership? What can a church do if it discovers that its pastor is a dictator?

5. How can Christians use written correspondence to promote the gospel more effectively? When should believers write "painful" letters to other believers? Should the letters always be signed?

6. Why are Christians often reluctant to forgive other believers? What can be done to change this attitude?

7. How can Satan take advantage of Christians? What types of thoughts originate from him?

3

The Superiority of the Gospel Ministry

II Corinthians 2:14—3:18

After defending his personal conduct (1:1–2:13), Paul moved into this second major section of the letter, a defense of his ministry (2:14–7:16). Actually, it takes the form of a parenthesis, between his concern over the absence of Titus at Troas and his joy over the coming of his friend at Macedonia (2:12–13; cf. 7:5–7).

Paul began his defense by comparing the content and results of his gospel message with that of the Judaizers, the false teachers who taught that obedience to the Mosaic Law, including circumcision, was necessary for salvation. The apostle frequently had to wrestle with these enemies of the gospel of grace (cf. Acts 15:1; Gal. 2:4; Phil. 3:2, 17–19). These false teachers had invaded the Corinthian assembly, which was split with personal dissension and immoral living, and had taken advantage of Paul's absence to discredit his ministry and apostleship. Now Paul had to defend the nature of his ministry to the very people who had benefited from his evangelization (Acts 18) and from his written correspondence.

To do so, he divided his defense into two parts. First, he contrasted himself with the false teachers and secondly, he compared his ministry with that of Moses, the human instrument in the giving of the law.

I. CONTRAST WITH THE FALSE TEACHERS (2:14–3:5)

Paul was amazed that his converts could be deceived by the faulty content and devious methods of the false teachers (cf. 11:4). In his opinion, his ministry was so radically different from the Judaizers that the churches should have recognized the apparent contrast instantaneously. But the believers did not, and the apostle had to fire sharp warnings at them. For example, to the Galatians he wrote: "O foolish Galatians, who hath bewitched you, that ye should not obey the truth" (Gal. 3:1, 3). He lamented: "I marvel that ye are so soon removed from him that called you into the grace of Christ unto another gospel" (Gal. 1:6). In this section, Paul outlined four major contrasts between his ministry and that of the false teachers.

A. In Results (2:14–16)

The church at Corinth was riddled with personal, moral, and doctrinal problems. In his first epistle, Paul had argued that the value of a man's work could be seen in its permanency (I Cor. 3:12–15). The false teachers charged that the poor spiritual condition of the Corinthians resulted from Paul's weak ministry of antinomianism.[1] They claimed that the apostle's interpretation of justification by grace through faith had issued in moral anarchy.

1. His success came from God (2:14)

Paul began this section with praise: "Now thanks be unto God." This optimistic outburst must be seen in contrast to the gloom and concern that he experienced in Ephesus, Troas, and Macedonia. The absence of Titus did not detract from the presence of God.

1. The word means "against legalism."

He was thankful for two reasons. *First,* God "always caused [him] to triumph in Christ." The apostle was not a victim, but a victor! The imagery behind the verb "causeth to triumph" *(thriambeuō)* is taken from the processions of ancient Roman emperors and generals who led the captives taken in battle and exposed them to the gaze of a cheering public. Paul saw himself as a member of Christ's army, enjoying the victory march as he followed his spiritual king. Christ predicted: "I will build my church; and the gates of hell shall not prevail against it" (Matt. 16:18). Paul knew that he had laid the foundation of the church at Corinth according to Christ's specifications; thus he remained convinced that his work would stand the test of time. Assured that he shared in Christ's triumphs over sin, death, legalism, and Satan, the apostle wrote:

> Blotting out the handwriting of ordinances that was against us, which was contrary to us, and took it out of the way, nailing it to his cross;
>
> And having spoiled principalities and powers, he made a show of them openly, *triumphing over them* in it (Col. 2:14–15).

Second, God used him to spread the knowledge of God to a pagan Roman world (2:14b). Robertson commented: "In a Roman triumph garlands of flowers scattered sweet odour and incense bearers dispensed perfumes. The knowledge of God is here the aroma which Paul had scattered like an incense bearer."[2] The apostle experienced the joy and victory of being a spokesman for God. He claimed the ancient promise: "So shall my word be that goeth forth out of my mouth: it shall not return unto me void, but it shall accomplish that which I please, and it shall prosper in the thing whereto I sent it" (Isa. 55:11).

2. A. T. Robertson, *Word Pictures in the New Testament,* 6 vols. (Nashville: Broadman Press, 1930-33), 4:218.

2. His ministry resulted in life or death (2:15–16)

Paul then equated his life and ministry as "a sweet savour of Christ." Someone has remarked that in spreading the fragrance of Christ the preacher will himself become fragrant (cf. Phil. 1:21). He radiated the same sweetness of spiritual life regardless of whether he was with "them that are saved" or with "them that perish."

He then noted: "To the one we are the savour of death unto death; and to the other the savour of life unto life" (2:16a). In the triumphal processions, the captives were chained together, sometimes even to the chariot wheels. As the fragrance of the incense permeated the parade route, it was a constant reminder to the captives that they had been defeated and to the victorious soldiers that they had won. The fragrance meant two different things to two different groups. Solomon observed that "death and life are in the power of the tongue" (Prov. 18:21). The apostle knew that those who accepted the redemptive message of Christ's death and resurrection which he proclaimed would be saved and that those who rejected it would remain in a state of spiritual death, perishing, and bound for hell.

Paul did not expect that everyone would respond to his gospel. No anointed prophet does. In speaking of the infant Christ, Simeon exclaimed: "Behold, this child is set for the fall and rising again of many in Israel" (Luke 2:34). Jesus Himself said: "Suppose ye that I am come to give peace on earth? I tell you, Nay; but rather division" (Luke 12:51).

Paul's question marked his awareness of his awesome responsibility: "And who is sufficient for these things?" (2:16b). When a preacher realizes that a person could be saved or condemned on the basis of his message, then he had better be sure about the truthfulness of his word and the purity of his motivation. He must draw his sufficiency from God, and not from himself. He must see himself as an instrument of the Holy Spirit to draw men to God (John 6:44; 15:26–27). No man, no matter how educated his mind and how polished his oratory, can convince another to become a Christian through mere human means (I Cor. 2:1–4).

B. In Methods (2:17)

1. Negatively (2:17a)

Paul claimed: "For we are not as many, which corrupt the word of God." He used the word "many" *(hoi polloi)* to refer to the large number of false teachers infiltrating and defiling the churches. Elsewhere, he warned: "For many walk, of whom I have told you often, and now tell you even weeping, that they are the enemies of the cross of Christ" (Phil. 3:18). Even in his day the apostle saw himself within the minority of faithful gospel preachers.

The apostates corrupted the oral and written word of God. The word "corrupt" *(kapēleuō)* was used of peddlers or hucksters who would sell damaged goods or lighten weight for personal gain. They were like vendors suspected of putting the best fruit on the top of a basket full of immature and bruised fruit. In a sense, they were men pleasers (Gal. 1:10).

2. Positively (2:17b)

Paul used four prepositional phrases to show his method of speaking. *First,* it was "of sincerity" (cf. 1:12). A huckster would disguise a crack in a pot by covering it over with dye or paint, but the apostle claimed that there were no flaws in his motivation. *Second,* it was "of God" *(ek theou).* The source of his apostolic authority and ministry came from God (Gal. 1:11–12). Like John the Baptist, he was "a man sent from God" (John 1:6). *Third,* his speaking was done "in the sight of God." There was nothing private about his life. God knew what he said, thought, and meant at all times. Paul welcomed this type of scrutiny (I Cor. 4:1–5; I Thess. 2:4). *Fourth,* it was done "in Christ." His ministry reflected his new spiritual position in Christ (II Cor. 5:17). The false teachers, on the other hand, were outside of Christ. They knew nothing of being "accepted in the beloved" (Eph. 1:6).

C. In Commendation (3:1–3)

Letters of commendation or introduction were frequently sent in New Testament times. The church at Jerusalem commended Judas and Silas via letter to the church at Antioch (Acts 15:22–31). The believers at Ephesus introduced Apollos to the Corinthian church in the same way (Acts 18:27). Paul commended Phebe to the church at Rome (Rom. 16:1–2), Timothy and Titus to the church at Corinth (I Cor. 16:10; II Cor. 8:23), and John Mark to the church at Colosse (Col. 4:10). Thus, letters were sent by churches and influential leaders to introduce lesser known people and to promote support for their respective ministries.

1. Paul did not need human commendation (3:1)

Paul was not against such letters for others, but he sensed no need to have them for himself. He rebelled against any suggestion that he had to be treated in the same way as lesser known itinerant preachers. He was not on equal terms with other itinerant preachers, especially the Judaizers who probably utilized such letters effectively. Paul knew that fact, and he wanted the church to know it also.

In a series of three questions, he pointed out that he had no need of human accreditation. First, there was no need for self-accreditation. He did not have to write a letter in which he listed his spiritual achievements. Second, there was no need for other churches to defend Paul to the church at Corinth. The reference to "some" shows that the itinerant preachers who came to Corinth brought with them letters of introduction (real or forged?) from other churches. Third, he did not want any letter of commendation from them.

2. Paul had divine commendation (3:2–3)

Paul now admitted that he had a unique epistle of commendation.[3] He mentioned five features about it. *First,* it was personal ("ye"). Paul's epistle was made of people, not of paper. The Corinthian believers themselves were his epistle.

Second, it was an internal epistle ("written in our hearts"). The names of the Corinthians were held in the hearts of Paul, Timothy, and Silas when they evangelized the city, and later in the heart of Titus.[4] The Corinthians had made an indelible impression upon the apostle's heart that could not be erased.

Third, his fervent attachment to them was "known and read of all men." His heart was an open book, not a closed diary. Other churches and preachers knew that Paul abundantly loved the church at Corinth (6:11; 7:2; 12:15).

Fourth, the Corinthians were actually "the epistle of Christ" written on his heart. The Savior was the author of

3. The word "epistle" is very emphatic in the sentence, standing first even though it is the predicate nominative.

4. The verb "written" is a perfect passive participle. This indicates that what was written once in the past stands written in the present. It cannot be erased.

this living letter. Others could look into the heart of Paul and see how Christ had impressed the Corinthians into his very being.

Fifth, the writing materials were unique. The church desired letters written with ink, but Christ had composed his living epistle with the Holy Spirit. The Spirit had produced His fruit through Paul, including genuine brotherly love (Gal. 5:22–23). In the old covenant period, God wrote the Ten Commandments with His finger on two tables of stone, but in the new covenant era, He writes on human hearts (Exod. 31:18; cf. Jer. 31:33; Ezek. 36:26–27).

D. In Ability (3:4–5)

1. Confidence in God (3:4)

Paul was not cocky or self-assured, but he did know that God had worked both in and through him. Hughes observed: "He who has, through Christ, received all things from God looks with confidence, through Christ, to God."[5] His confidence ("such trust") was based upon the operation of God described in the previous two verses. It was a present possession ("we have") obtained through divine means ("through Christ"). It was a confidence directed toward God and not toward self ("to God-ward").

2. Sufficiency from God (3:5)

Paul was quick to credit his abilities and accomplishments to God. He repudiated self-dependence for the achievements of his ministry. He recognized that his sufficiency to preach came from God. Paul acknowledged

5. Philip E. Hughes, *The Second Epistle to the Corinthians,* New International Commentary on the New Testament (Grand Rapids: Wm. B. Eerdmans Publishing Co., 1962), p. 92.

that God was the source of his physical life and strength, his spiritual life, his speech, and his mental logic. Earlier he had told them: "But by the grace of God I am what I am: and his grace which was bestowed upon me was not in vain; but I laboured more abundantly than they all: yet not I, but the grace of God which was with me" (I Cor. 15:10).

II. CONTRAST WITH MOSES (3:6–18)

The Judaizers were self-appointed, false apostles. After Paul contrasted his accreditation with theirs, he then sought to demonstrate the difference between his ministry and their message. He proclaimed grace, whereas they taught that obedience to the law of Moses was necessary for justification and sanctification. It was imperative, therefore, for Paul to compare himself, the apostle to the Gentiles, with Moses, the giver of the law to Israel.

A. The Two Covenants (3:6–11)

Is the new covenant simply a further revelation of the old, or is it a replacement? Is the new only an internal expression of the old? Are men to be saved through conformity to both the old and the new? In the following contrasts, Paul clearly defined the radical difference between the two covenants.

1. Old or new (3:6a)

Almost six centuries before Christ, God promised: "Behold, the days come, saith the Lord, that I will make a new covenant with the house of Israel, and with the house of Judah: Not according to the covenant that I made with their fathers in the day that I took them out of the land of Egypt" (Jer. 31:31–32). Christ, on the night before His crucifixion, instituted the ordinance of the Lord's Supper and explained the meaning of the wine: "For this is my blood of the new testament, which is shed for many for the remission of sins" (Matt. 26:28).[6] The blood of the Passover lamb became the basis of the old covenant, whereas the blood of Jesus Christ shed on the cross of Calvary became the foundation of the new.

The Book of Hebrews presents the priesthood of Christ as superior to that of the Jewish priests in five ways: position (4:14–16), order (5:1–7:28), covenant (8:1–13), sanctuary (9:1–11), and sacrifice (9:12–10:18). The writer affirmed:

> But now hath [Christ] obtained a more excellent ministry, by how much also he is the mediator of a *better covenant*, which was established upon *better promises*.
>
> But if that *first covenant* had been faultless, then should no place have been sought for the *second* (Heb. 8:6–7).

He then concluded: "In that he saith, a new covenant, he hath made the first old. Now that which decayeth and waxeth old is ready to vanish away" (Heb. 8:13).

Paul claimed that the law was temporary and that "it was added because of transgressions, till the seed should come to whom the promise was made" (Gal. 3:19). That "seed" was Christ (Gal. 3:16). When a person has come to faith in Christ, he is no longer under the law (Rom. 6:14; Gal. 3:25).

Since Christ's ministry in the new covenant was better to that of the priests in the old, Paul knew that his ministry was superior to that of the Judaizers. He knew that God "made [him] able."[7] The usage of the past tense refers to the definite call of God into the ministry.

6. Both "covenant" and "testament" come from the same Greek word *diathēkē*.

7. The verb "made able" *(hikanōsen)* and the noun "sufficiency" *(hikanotēs)* are from the same Greek root.

Mount Sinai, as viewed from the Plain of Sinai.

2. Letter or spirit (3:6b)

The old covenant can be read; the new can be lived. The old was contained in Hebrew letters written on stones and later in the Pentateuch, but the new is inscribed on the human spirit by the Holy Spirit (3:3). God promised: "And I will put my spirit within you, and cause you to walk in my statutes, and ye shall keep my judgments, and do them" (Ezek. 36:26). Under the old covenant, conformity to the moral law of God was imposed from outside, whereas in the new, obedience is generated from within the person.

3. Kills or gives life (3:6b)

The reason why the law "kills" is because no person has within himself the ability to keep it. Paul wrote:

> For I was alive without the law once: but when the commandment came, sin revived, and I died.
> And the commandment, which was ordained to life, I found to be unto death.
> For sin, taking occasion by the commandment, deceived me, and by it slew me (Rom. 7:9–11).

To avoid the curse and the judgment through breaking a law, a person must keep the commandments without exception (Gal. 3:10). If he breaks just one commandment once, he is morally culpable for both physical and eternal death (James 2:10–11).

On the other hand, the new covenant "giveth life." Jesus remarked: "It is the spirit that quickeneth; the flesh profiteth nothing: the words that I speak unto you, they are spirit, and they are life" (John 6:63).

4. Ministration of death or spirit (3:7a)

If a minister preached only the law of Moses, no one would be saved. The law of the old covenant did not show men how to be right before God; rather it demonstrated how holy God is and how sinful men are. Paul said that "the law is holy, and the commandment holy, and just, and good" (Rom. 7:12). He then added: "Was then that which is good made death unto me? God forbid. But sin, that it might appear sin, working death in me by that which is good; that sin by the commandment might become exceeding sinful" (Rom. 7:13). Through the old covenant, man perceives his state of spiritual death but remains incapable of delivering himself.

When the new covenant of Christ's redemptive death and resurrection is proclaimed, however, men can pass from death unto life through the new birth (John 3:5; 5:24). All men who are dead in trespasses and sins can be quickened (made alive) only by grace through faith (Eph. 2:1–8).

5. Temporary or permanent glory (3:7–11)

The glory of God is the manifestation of His character and purpose. The law, even though it was the ministration of death, was "glorious" in that it reflected the holiness of God. The gospel message, as the ministration of the spirit, is "rather [more] glorious" because it reveals the love, grace, mercy, and forgiveness of God. It is true that "the law was given by Moses, but grace and truth came by Jesus Christ" (John 1:17; cf. 1:14).

Paul claimed that the glory of the new covenant was superior through the usage of key comparative phrases: "rather [more] glorious" (3:8); "much more" (3:9); "exceed in glory" (3:9); "that excelleth" (3:10); and "that which remaineth" (3:10).

He twice mentioned that the glory of the law was being "done away" (3:7, 11). The glory of the law was manifested in the glory of [Moses'] countenance" (3:7). This outward change in appearance occurred when Moses was on Mount Sinai for forty days at the time God gave the law (Exod. 34:29–35). Moses, however, was unaware that the skin of his face shone both while he was on the mountain and after he descended. This reflected glory gradually diminished until his face had a natural appearance once again. This event in the life of Moses anticipated the decline of the glory of the law (Gal. 3:19–25).

When Moses came down from Mount Sinai, "the children of Israel could not stedfastly behold" his face (3:7, 13). "They were afraid to come nigh him" (Exod. 34:30). Whenever Moses spoke to them, he had to veil his face to alleviate their fear. Men are repulsed by the glory of the law, but they are attracted by the glory of the new covenant.

6. Condemnation or righteousness (3:9)

The law tells men what they should do, but the gospel tells men what Christ has done. The law demands righteousness, but the gospel gives righteousness. Men approach the law out of fear because they stand condemned before it, but when they appropriate the gospel through faith, they are lovingly thankful to God. Under the old covenant, men approached a throne of judgment, but in the new, they came boldly to the throne of grace (Heb. 4:16).

B. The Two Ministries (3:12–16)

All would agree that Christ had a ministry superior to that of Moses (Heb. 3:1–6). But did Paul also have a greater ministry than that of the law giver? In the progressive revelation of the divine redemptive program, the apostle actually did. His superiority is seen in two ways.

1. In proclamation (3:12–13)

The basis of his ministry was "hope," a present conviction ("we have") that all of the promises of the new covenant would be fulfilled in his life. The new covenant is unconditional, dependent only upon God's faithfulness to His pledged word for completion; but the old covenant was conditional, based upon man's obedience for fulfillment (Exod. 19:5–6; cf. 19:8). Elsewhere, Paul wrote: "For we are saved by hope: but hope that is seen is not hope: for what a man seeth, why doth he yet hope for? But if we hope for that we see not, then do with patience wait for it" (Rom. 8:24–25). The life of hope is evidenced by a walk of faith.

Because of his assurance, Paul used "great plainness of speech." He addressed his congregation courageously and clearly. Without reservation, he could tell them why they were lost and what they needed to do to be saved. He could explain the total redemptive program of the ages and point them to the ultimate climax at the coming of Christ.

Moses, on the other hand, veiled himself when he spoke. The people were afraid to view his shining face. As they were unable to see the glory of his radiant countenance come to an end, neither were they able to see that the glory of the law would end with the advent of Christ. The nation, through the system of blood sacrifices, could not see that offerings would be fulfilled in the substitutionary death of Jesus Christ. The Savior Himself said: "Think not that I am come to destroy the law, or the prophets: I am not come to destroy, but to fulfil" (Matt. 5:17). Paul added that "Christ is the end of the law for righteousness to every one that believeth" (Rom. 10:4).

2. In response (3:14–16)

The proclamation of the law produces and confirms blindness, whereas the preaching of the gospel removes blindness. The minds of the Jews "were blinded" (literally, "were hardened," *epōrōthe).*[8] The thoughts of their minds *(noēmata)* were callused, or petrified. Their spiritual hardness was caused by their own sin and stubbornness (John 9:39–41; Heb. 3:8), controlled by Satan (4:4), and confirmed by God (Isa. 6:9–10; cf. John 12:38–41; Rom. 11:7–8).

When Moses spoke to the people, the veil was upon his face, but when the law of Moses was later read, the veil was upon the hearts of the individual Jews and of national Israel. In both cases, the people could not see the glory of God, namely the glory of Jesus Christ. Jesus challenged His generation: "Search the scriptures; for in them ye think ye have eternal life: and they are they which testify of me"

8. This is a different word than that later used *(etuphlōse;* 4:4).

(John 5:39). He later concluded: "For had ye believed Moses, ye would have believed me: for he wrote of me. But if ye believe not his writings, how shall ye believe my words?" (John 5:46–47). In Paul's day, the situation had not changed ("until this day"), and it is still true in this era.

When a person stops trusting in his effort to keep the law and starts to believe in God's provision, then "the veil is done away in Christ." Just as Moses removed the veil when he was in the presence of the Lord, so the veil will be lifted from the hearts of Jews when they see the fulfillment of the law's demands in the person and redemptive work of Christ (Rom. 10:1–13). They need to have their spiritual understanding opened by Christ to see him in the Old Testament (Luke 24:25–27; 44–45).

Within Israel today, a "remnant according to the election of grace" has obtained the promised blessings of the Old Testament covenants, but the great majority is still blinded (Rom. 11:5–8). It was Paul's privilege to introduce many Jews to the promised Messiah. He also anticipated a future time when national Israel would accept Jesus as their Messiah and God ("when it shall turn to the Lord").[9] After the church age ("the fullness of the Gentiles") is over, then "all Israel shall be saved" (Rom. 11:25–26). At the second coming of Christ to the earth, Israel will turn to Him. At that time, the new covenant will be fulfilled in Israel: "A new heart also will I give you, and a new spirit will I put within you: and I will take away the stony heart out of your flesh, and I will give you an heart of flesh" (Ezek. 36:26).

9. The word "it" is not in the Greek. The verb is third person singular. This means that the subject of the verb could be masculine ("he"), feminine ("she"), or neuter ("it"). In all cases, the antecedent of the pronoun must be speculated upon: the individual Jew, the nation, or the heart.

C. The Two Effects (3:17–18)

The proclamation of the law produced both fear and blindness. The false teaching of the Judaizers did the same. Paul's ministry, however, resulted in two major spiritual benefits.

1. It produces liberty (3:17)

Christ said: "If the Son therefore shall make you free, ye shall be free indeed" (John 8:36). All men are "under sin," under its penalty, power, and effects (Rom. 3:9). They are slaves to sin. There is no way that men can work to gain their spiritual freedom. Paul asserted: "Therefore by the deeds of the law there shall no flesh be justified in his sight" (Rom. 3:20). They are under the condemnation of the broken moral law of God. Their deliverance had to come from someone who was not himself trapped in the same predicament. This is why God became man:

> But when the fulness of the time was come, God set forth his Son, made of a woman, made under the law,
> To redeem them that were under the law, that we might receive the adoption of sons.
> And because ye are sons, God hath sent forth the Spirit of his Son into your hearts, crying, Abba, Father.
> Wherefore thou art no more a servant, but a son; and if a son, then an heir of God through Christ (Gal. 4:4–7).

After a person has been justified by faith in Christ, he should walk under the control of the indwelling Holy Spirit rather than under the legalistic regulations of the Mosaic law (Gal. 5:16, 22–23; Col. 2:14–3:4).[10] He is no

10. Some key concepts about the doctrine of the Holy Spirit are found in this verse. Just as the Father and the Son are one in essence (John 10:30), so are the Son and the Spirit ("the Lord is that Spirit"). The Holy Spirit can be designated either as the Spirit of the Father (Eph. 4:30) or the Spirit of the Son (Rom. 8:9) because the Spirit has been sent forth by both the Father and the Son (John 14:26; 15:26).

longer "under the law, but under grace" (Rom. 6:14–15). Paul admonished: "Stand fast therefore in the liberty wherewith Christ hath made us free, and be not entangled again with the yoke of bondage" (Gal. 5:1).

The gospel produces liberty from bondage to sin and to the law. Someone has said that "Christ has set us free to become all we were meant to be."

2. It produces Christ-likeness (3:18)

The gospel produces internal, spiritual transformation whereas the law produced external, physical regulation. The likeness of God upon Moses was outward, and it gradually diminished. Moses viewed the glory of God only upon the mountain.

On the other hand, the Christian can see the glory of God every day in the Scriptures ("glass," literally "mirror"). Just as Moses viewed the glory with unveiled face, so the believer with "open face" (literally, "unveiled face") can do the same. The believer becomes Godlike as the Spirit of God gradually produces His fruit through him (Gal. 5:22–23). The goal of every child of God should be to emulate the experience of the apostle: "For to me to live is Christ" (Phil. 1:21; cf. Col. 3:1–4).

QUESTIONS FOR DISCUSSION

1. In their ministries, why do Christians sense defeat more than triumph? How can this perspective be corrected?

2. Are professing evangelicals corrupting or huckstering the gospel today? If so, in what ways? How can this perversion be stopped?

3. What types of commendation occur today? Is it good or bad? Should it be encouraged?

4. Where does confidence in self end and trust in God begin? Does seminary training promote self-sufficiency?

5. Is legalism a problem today in evangelical churches? Do Christians understand the teachings of living by grace?

6. How can Jewish people be effectively reached with the gospel? Should separate mission boards for Jewish witness be in existence?

7. Are believers more interested in looking like Christians than being Christian? How can an emphasis be put on inward character rather than outward conformity?

4

The Glory of the Gospel Ministry

II Corinthians 4

Paul was thankful that he was a minister, and testified: "And I thank Christ Jesus our Lord, who hath enabled me, for that he counted me faithful, putting me into the ministry" (I Tim. 1:12). To him, the glory of the ministry was in its message, in its enablement, and in its results. He looked upon the "glorious gospel" as a sacred trust (I Tim. 1:11). In spite of all the difficulties that he encountered, Paul rejoiced in what God had done through his life. He looked forward with eager anticipation to future blessings. In this chapter, the apostle enumerated both the problems that he faced and the victories that were won.

I. THE PROBLEMS OF THE MINISTRY (4:1–4)

Jesus never promised that His followers would have an easy time in this life. To the scribe who bragged that he would follow the Lord anywhere, Christ cautioned: "The foxes have holes, and the birds of the air have nests; but the Son of man hath not where to lay his head" (Matt. 8:20). God does not recruit prospective ministers with the allurement of popular acclaim or financial security. Paul knew that. He stated concerning the gospel: "Whereunto I am appointed a preacher, and an apostle, and a teacher of the Gentiles. For the which cause I also suffer these things: Nevertheless I am not ashamed" (II Tim. 1:11–12). Future ministers should realize that there will be problems ahead in the performance of their service. In this section, Paul mentioned three.

A. Emotional Weakness (4:1)

Twice in this chapter, the apostle boldly claimed that he did not faint (4:1, 16). The verb "to faint" means to give in to evil, to behave badly, or to lose courage *(ekkakeō)*. He was not a faint-hearted coward. Later, he encouraged Timothy at a time when the young associate was timid: ". . . stir up the gift of God. . . . For God hath not given us the spirit of fear; but of power, and of love, and of a sound mind" (II Tim. 1:6–7). Pressures will mount, but the wise minister will learn to cast his anxieties upon God and will prayerfully bathe himself in the peace of God, which can protect his mental and emotional stability (Phil. 4:6–7; I Peter 5:7). One way in which Satan consumes the effectiveness of preachers and Christians is through worry (I Peter 5:8; cf. 5:7).

Paul listed two reasons for not giving in to pressure. *First,* he knew that he had been given "this ministry." When God calls, He enables. The sufficiency of God is available in all situations (3:6)–for courage and ability to speak and for emotional support regardless of results. *Second,* he knew that he had "received mercy" both for salvation and service. He knew that before a holy God he once was "a blasphemer, and a persecutor, and injurious" (I Tim. 1:13). He knew that he deserved the judgment of God, but God mercifully had saved him. He knew that with God's help he would not faint, regardless of the internal and external pressures that he bore.

B. Faulty Motivation (4:2)

To be effective, a pastor must have integrity, faith, and a good conscience (I Tim. 1:18–19). He should be blameless (I Tim. 3:1). He should have a "good report of all men, and of the truth itself" (III John v. 12). Paul constantly tested his motivations to make sure that they manifested these holy standards.

1. Negative goals (4:2a)

He firmly rejected three areas of faulty motivation that marked the false teachers. *First,* he "renounced the hidden things of dishonesty." The word for "dishonesty" literally means "shame" *(aischunē).* He did not handle holy things with unclean hands or an impure heart (cf. Hag. 2:10–14). The manner of life must support the message. Elsewhere, he wrote: "And have no fellowship with the unfruitful works of darkness, but rather reprove them. For it is a shame even to speak of those things which are done of them in secret" (Eph. 5:11–12). A minister should not be ashamed to have his life investigated. He must determine to be pure in his life at all times.

Second, he did not walk "in craftiness." A crafty person will do anything, good or bad, to achieve his desired goal. Paul did not believe that the end justified the means. A godly man must use godly methods to accomplish godly results.

Third, he did not "handle the word of God deceitfully." He did not misrepresent the gospel message to others. He told men what they needed to hear, not what they wanted to hear. The Greek concept behind "deceit" is to catch fish with bait. He did not try to trick people into the kingdom of God.

2. Positive goals (4:2b)

Paul determined to manifest "the truth" regardless of the outcome. All believers should "speak the truth in love" (Eph. 4:15), love for the sake of truth (II John vv. 1–2), and walk in truth (II John v. 4). Christ claimed to be the truth (John 14:6), and whatever is truth will conform to His manner of behavior and proclamation.

He wanted to have pure motivations both before men ("every man's conscience") and God ("in the sight of God"). Sincerity and purity must mark the personal relationships of the minister.

It is possible for a person to preach the right message but with a wrong motivation. Paul commented: "Some indeed preach Christ even of envy and strife . . . of contention, not sincerely, supposing to add affliction to my bonds" (Phil. 1:15–16). We can rejoice that Christ is preached, but we cannot rejoice in the faulty motivation. At the judgment seat of Christ, men will be judged for their message, methods, and motivation (I Cor. 4:5).

C. Satanic Opposition (4:3–4)

There is a spiritual warfare going on behind human activities. From the time when he first attempted to usurp divine authority, Satan has continued to oppose the purposes of God. Satan hates God, the redemptive message, gospel ministers, and all other believers. Paul warned all believers:

> Put on the whole armour of God, that ye may be able to stand against the wiles of the devil.
>
> For we wrestle not against flesh and blood, but against principalities, against powers, against the rulers of the darkness of this world, against spiritual wickedness in high places (Eph. 6:11–12).

Paul indicated that Satan on two occasions had "hindered" his movements to preach at Thessalonica (I Thess. 2:18).

1. Victims of the opposition (4:3–4a)

They are described in four ways. *First,* they "are lost" (cf. Luke 19:10). Literally, they "are perishing" (cf. I Cor. 1:18). They are not perishing because they do not perceive the gospel message, but it is hidden to them because they are already perishing. Boyer wrote: "The word 'perish' does not indicate extinction, but ruin; not loss of *being,* but loss of *well-being.*"[1] The "lost" are unsaved sinners who need to be redeemed.

Second, the gospel "is hid to them."[2] This does not mean that the gospel is hidden and that the unsaved cannot find it. Rather, it exists in a veiled state to them. The word "hid" *(kekalummenon)* is from the same Greek root as "veil" *(kalumma).* The spiritual veil is not over the gospel, because the redemptive message can be clearly seen (cf. 3:12). Instead, the veil is over the minds of the lost. Just as the veil must be taken off the heart of Israel so that the covenant nation can see Christ in the Old Testament, so the veil must be lifted off the minds of the unsaved so that they might see the Savior in the gospel message.[3]

Third, their "minds" have been "blinded" by Satan. The gospel is to the "Jews a stumblingblock, and unto the Greeks foolishness" (I Cor. 1:23). The Jews expected the

1. James L. Boyer, *For a World Like Ours* (Grand Rapids: Baker Book House, 1972), p. 34.

2. The verbs "be hid" and "is hid" are the translations of *esti kekalummenon,* the periphrastic construction of the perfect passive participle with the present form of *eimi.* It means that a past action stands as a present reality.

3. The term "our gospel" means "the gospel which we preached." The word "our" *(hēmōn)* is the grammatical subjective genitive.

Messiah to bring political victory and live forever (Matt. 27:42; John 12:34). The Gentiles viewed a crucified person as morally offensive and as an evidence of physical weakness. They denied that the blood of such a person could remove sin, give righteousness, and guarantee hope beyond the grave. To them, the gospel message was absurd.

Fourth, they "believe not." To be saved, a sinner must believe on Christ (Acts 16:31). Their unbelief shows that they were already in a position of spiritual condemnation before God (John 3:18).

2. Source of the opposition (4:4a)

Satan is here called "the god of this world" (literally, "of this age"; *aiōnos).* Jesus identified him as "the prince of this world" *(kosmou;* John 12:31; 14:30; 16:11). Paul later named him as "the prince of the power of the air, the spirit that now worketh in the children of disobedience" (Eph. 2:2). God is really "the King eternal," literally "the King of the ages" (I Tim. 1:17), but He has permitted Satan to have power in this age only.

All unsaved men are situated in the lap of the wicked one (I John 5:19).[4] When men are converted, they are delivered "from the power of darkness" (Col. 1:13).

3. Purpose of the opposition (4:4b)

Satan wants the lost to remain in a veiled state of spiritual darkness. Just as Israel could not see the glory of God radiating from the countenance of Moses because of the veil over his head, so the unsaved cannot see the glory of Christ in the gospel message because their minds are

4. The phrase "in wickedness" literally means "in the wicked one" *(en tōi ponērōi).*

blinded and veiled. The believer can see the glory of Christ in the Scriptures, but the unsaved cannot (3:18).

Satan does not want sinners to recognize Jesus Christ as God. As "the image of God," Christ could say: "He that hath seen me hath seen the Father" (John 14:19). All that God the Father is, God the Son is (John 10:30; Col. 1:15; Heb. 1:3).

II. THE VICTORIES OF THE MINISTRY (4:5–18)

The child of God can triumph against the problems created by self, by others, and by Satan. The ecstasy of spiritual victory overcomes the agony of opposition. In this section, the apostle described five types of victory.

A. Light Over Darkness (4:5–6)

How can a minister overcome Satanic blindness? How can a man defeat the wicked one?

1. The object of preaching (4:5)

The solution is to "preach" over and over.[5] The unsaved do not need to see miracles or to hear logical debates, but they do need to hear a clear proclamation of the gospel message of the redeeming grace of God. Paul emphasized three areas in his preaching.

First, he did not preach himself. No man can save another man. Robertson remarked that the preaching of self is "surely as poor and disgusting a topic as a preacher can find."[6] The false teachers, unfortunately, did just that (10:12).

5. The verb is in the present tense.

6. A. T. Robertson, *Word Pictures in the New Testament,* 6 vols. (Nashville: Broadman Press, 1931), 4:225.

Second, he preached "Christ Jesus the Lord." The apostle proclaimed that God had become man in Christ and that the divine-human person had been crucified for sins and raised again for justification (Rom. 4:25; 10:9–10).

Third, his associates and he declared themselves "your servants for Jesus' sake." Paul served others; he did not expect others to serve him. He used his apostolic prerogatives as greater opportunities for ministry, not for selfish gratification.

2. The reason for preaching (4:6)

Darkness can only be dispelled by the entrance of light. After the initial creation of matter, "darkness was upon the face of the deep" (Gen. 1:2). On that first day, God said, "Let there be light: and there was light" (Gen. 1:3). Only God could have removed that physical darkness.

Also, only God can remove spiritual darkness. For the veil and the blindness of sinful hearts to be taken away, God must sovereignly say: "Let there be light." Unsaved men "walk in the vanity of their mind, having the understanding darkened, being alienated from the life of God through the ignorance that is in them, because of the blindness of their heart" (Eph. 4:17–18). When men are born again, they become "enlightened" (Heb. 6:4).

Paul knew that God had "shined" in his heart (Gal. 1:15–16). On the road to Damascus, he was blinded physically but enlightened spiritually. He then knew that others could be enlightened if he would only permit the glory of Christ who was within him to shine through him. By becoming a humble servant, Christ could be manifested through his person and preaching. Christ said to Paul: ". . . now I send thee, to open their eyes, and to turn them from darkness to light, and from the power of Satan unto

God, that they may receive forgiveness of sins, and inheritance among them which are sanctified by faith that is in me" (Acts 26:17–18). As a true servant, Paul could honestly report to all men: "I was not disobedient unto the heavenly vision" (Acts 26:19). He had seen thousands come to Christ. It was no wonder that Satan viciously opposed him.

B. Power Over Weakness (4:7)

Paul knew his limitations, but he also knew the power of God. He had his weaknesses, but he was aware that the infinite God had none.

1. The possession of a treasure

It was a present possession ("we have"). Believers have an inheritance reserved in heaven (I Peter 1:4), but they also possess spiritual wealth now.

It is a spiritual "treasure." The usage of the adjective "this" refers to "the light of the knowledge of the glory of God in the face of Jesus Christ" (4:6). Believers are instructed to lay up treasures in heaven (Matt. 6:19–21), but this treasure has been deposited by God within the Christian's present body.

The treasure is found within "earthen vessels."[7] The body is often called a vessel (I Thess. 4:4; I Peter 3:7). Paul knew that he was a "chosen vessel" (Acts 9:15). It is "earthen" in that the human body is weak, corruptible, and mortal. It was formed out of the dust of the ground, and it returns to dust at death (Gen. 2:7; 3:19). Men are like clay pots fashioned by the divine potter (Rom. 9:20–22). The paradox is that inestimable wealth has

7. The word "earthen" comes from the Greek *ostraca,* a word used for common clay jars and for broken pieces used as writing pads.

been placed within inexpensive containers. It is like precious jewels stored in a coffee can.

2. The purpose of the possession

As there is little strength in earthen pots, there is no intrinsic spiritual ability in men who are the containers of divine treasure. The weakness of men further demonstrates that "the excellency of the power" must be "of God." Gideon learned this lesson when his army, reduced to three hundred, beseiged the Midianites with weapons of trumpets and burning lamps within clay pots (Judg. 7:16). Just as the pots had to be broken to let the lamps shine, so believers must be broken to manifest the light of God through them.

C. Encouragement Over Discouragement (4:8–9)

In warfare, a victorious army suffers battle casualties. In a championship boxing match, the winner hurts from the punches of his opponent. In the same sense, Paul had endured hardness as a good soldier, and he had won (II Tim. 2:3). He had received Satan's blows, but he had survived victorious.

In a series of four contrasts, Paul described the agony of conflict and the victory through survival that marked his life and ministry.[8]

1. In trouble (4:8a)

He was "troubled on every side, yet not distressed." He was pressed as grapes trodden in a winepress. He was squeezed, but he was not crushed or broken. Tasker relates the imagery of "a combatant who gives his opponent little

8. The contrasts are given in a series of present passive participles set off by the strong adversative "but" *(alla).*

room for action, but is unable to drive him into a corner where no movement is possible."[9] Later, the apostle reiterated the time when he was trapped within the city of Damascus and how he escaped in a basket let down through a window in the wall (11:32–33).

2. In perplexity (4:8b)

He was "perplexed, but not in despair."[10] Many times he felt lost or confused with no way to go, but he did not lose sight of God's care.

3. In persecution (4:9a)

He was "persecuted, but not forsaken." Wherever Paul went, he was pursued. Although he was hunted down as an animal, God never left Paul to go it alone.

4. In setbacks (4:9b)

He was "cast down, but not destroyed." He was knocked down, but he was never knocked out. He got up and kept going. He never quit. In this contrast, the apostle may have referred to the time when he was stoned at Lystra and left for dead (Acts 14:19–20). But God revived him; he arose the next day and continued on his preaching journey.

Paul realized that when he came to the end of his resources God began to manifest His resources. He later explained: "Therefore I take pleasure in infirmities, in reproaches, in necessities, in persecutions, in distresses for

9. R.V.G. Tasker, *The Second Epistle of Paul to the Corinthians*, Tyndale New Testament Commentaries (Grand Rapids: Wm. B. Eerdmans Publishing Co., 1960), p. 73.

10. Here is a play on words with the same verb being used twice: *aporoumenoi* and *exaporoumenoi.*

Christ's sake: for when I am weak, then am I strong" (12:10). All believers should likewise be encouraged by the all-inclusive promise of God: "My grace is sufficient for thee: for my strength is made perfect in weakness" (12:9).

D. Life Over Death (4:10–12)

Christ often contrasted life and death to illustrate the basic principle of spirituality and the necessity for His own crucifixion:

> Except a corn of wheat fall into the ground and die, it abideth alone: but if it die, it bringeth forth much fruit.
>
> He that loveth his life shall lose it; and he that hateth his life in this world shall keep it unto life eternal (John 12:24–25).

Paul recognized and practiced this concept when he testified: "I am crucified with Christ: nevertheless I live; yet not I, but Christ liveth in me: and the life which I now live in the flesh I live by the faith of the Son of God, who loved me, and gave himself for me (Gal. 2:20).

1. His dying

In these verses, Paul referred three times to the concept of dying. He said that he was "bearing about in the body the dying of the Lord Jesus (4:10), that he was "delivered unto death for Jesus' sake" (4:11), and that "death worketh in us" (4:12). He earlier had mentioned his deliverance from death threats (1:8–10), but here he was elaborating upon the death process that was operating in his life because of his strenuous service for others. Even Christ became fatigued in His earthly labors.

Also, Paul confronted the possibility of death almost daily. When he arose in the morning, he did not know whether he would go to bed that night. Elsewhere, he wrote: "For thy sake we are killed all the day long; we are accounted as sheep for the slaughter" (Rom. 8:36).

2. His living

In these verses, he also referred three times to the concept of living. Twice, he mentioned that the purpose of his dying was that "the life also of Jesus might be made manifest" in him (4:10–11). In a spiritual sense, Paul experienced the vitality of resurrection power to execute his ministry (Phil. 3:10). Every day he walked in newness of life (Rom. 6:4–6).

Paul also referred to life in his readers ("life in you"; 4:12). Just as Christ's death produced life in others, the apostle knew that his physical sufferings would encourage spiritual life in others. In this sense, he was identified with the Savior in His death and resurrection.

E. Faith Over Sight (4:13–18)

The Bible defines faith as "the substance of things hoped for, the evidence of things not seen" (Heb. 11:1). The writer of Hebrews stated that "without faith it is impossible to please" God (Heb. 11:6). The godly men of the Old Testament era walked and triumphed by faith, not by sight. And so did Paul.

1. Faith gave him speech (4:13)

Those with genuine faith are not ashamed to speak of their Christian experience. At conversion, "man believeth unto righteousness; and with the mouth confession is made unto salvation" (Rom. 10:10). After conversion, the testimony of faith should continue.

This is an Old Testament principle as well (Ps. 116:10). Paul had "the same spirit of faith" as the ancient Hebrews. The same Holy Spirit indwelt him, and he had the same disposition to tell others about his convictions.

Paul did not just occasionally witness; he declared the riches of Christ all of the time. It became part of his lifestyle. He commanded Timothy: "Preach the word; be instant in season, out of season" (II Tim. 4:2). He seldom voiced his opinions or doubts; rather, he proclaimed the convictions of his heart. He knew whom he believed and he knew what he believed. Paul found that his faith was too much to keep to himself. He had to share it with others.

2. Faith gave him assurance (4:14)

The participle "knowing" *(eidotes)* indicates a firm conviction of heart created by the teaching ministry of the Holy Spirit. He did not know these truths through observation or the instruction of others. Three persuasions are listed.

First, he believed that God had "raised up the Lord Jesus" from the dead (4:14a). Earlier, he had mentioned that his trust was "in God which raiseth the dead" (1:9). Before his conversion, he was convinced that Jesus was an imposter and that his body had been stolen from the tomb by the disciples. When the resurrected Christ appeared to him, his convictions radically changed (I Cor. 15:8–11). His faith, thus, was in the omnipotent God.

Second, he believed that in the future God would raise him from the dead (4:14b). On other, earlier occasions, the apostle expressed the conviction that Christ could come in his lifetime and that he would receive a new body through translation rather than through resurrection (I Cor. 15:51–52). He also believed that Christ might not come during his own lifetime. In that case, he would be among the dead in Christ who would be resurrected at the return of the Lord (I Thess. 4:13–18).

Third, he believed that God would present both the Corinthian believers and himself in heaven (4:14c). The presentation is of the mystical body of Christ, the true church, to Jesus Christ at the marriage of the Lamb (Rev. 19:7–8). He commented elsewhere:

> Husbands, love your wives, even as Christ also loved the church, and gave himself for it;
> That he might sanctify and cleanse it with the washing of water by the word,
> That he might present it to himself a glorious church, not having spot, or wrinkle, or any such thing; but that it should be holy and without blemish (Eph. 5:25–27).

As a minister, he knew that he was an instrument of God to promote purity within the churches (Col. 1:22–23). He desired to present the Corinthians "as a chaste virgin to Christ" (11:2).

3. Faith gave him endurance (4:15)

Endurance outwardly expresses inward faith. Four aspects of endurance are enumerated here.

First, he gladly endured that others might benefit ("all things are for your sakes"). Paul reflected the spirit of Christ, who endured the cross for others.

Second, he endured by the "abundant grace" of God. The grace of God not only saves but also sustains. All believers have received "grace for grace" (John 1:16), new grace for each new need.

Third, he endured that other believers would thank God for what He was doing in his life and in theirs. Christians rejoice when through failures and hardships God brings beauty out of ashes and triumph out of tragedy.

Fourth, he endured for "the glory of God." The Westminster Catechism states that the primary purpose and goal of man is to glorify God and to enjoy Him forever. The glorification of God can occur in times of difficulty as well as in the periods of peace.

4. Faith gave him strength (4:16)

Physically Paul grew weaker, but spiritually he grew stronger. The "outward man" is the mortal, corruptible body, deteriorating from the effects of sin and persecution. Paul did not expect to retain his health and strength throughout his lifetime.

His self ("the inward man"), however, was constantly being renewed. The strength of the inner self overcame the weakness of the outward man. This inner renewal caused him not to faint under the burden of physical and emotional distress. He confessed elsewhere: "For I reckon that the sufferings of this present time are not worthy to be compared with the glory which shall be revealed in us" (Rom. 8:18).

5. Faith gave him vision (4:17–18)

These two verses present five contrasts: "light" with "weight," "affliction" with "glory," "moment" with "eternal," "seen" with "not seen," and "temporal" with "eternal." They compare present experiences with future expectations. Paul knew that the scales would tip in favor of the future. He commanded: "Set your affection on things above, not on things on the earth" (Col. 3:2). Similarly, Jesus admonished: "Lay not up for yourselves treasures upon earth. . . . But lay up for yourselves treasures in heaven. . . . For where your treasure is, there will your heart be also" (Matt. 6:19–21).

Paul practiced what he preached. He viewed his physical problems ("light affliction") as temporary ("for a moment"). His difficulties, though light (relatively speaking), were not slight; they were severe (4:8–9).

He viewed them as a necessary means to a glorious end (4:17b). Paul believed and experienced the truth of this oft quoted verse: "And we know that all things work together for good to them that love God, to them who are the called according to his purpose" (Rom. 8:28).

He set his spiritual vision on eternal goals (4:18). Again, faith is "the evidence of things not seen" (Heb. 11:1). Peter wrote about the heavenly Christ: "Whom having not seen, ye love; in whom, though now ye see him not, yet believing, ye rejoice with joy unspeakable and full of glory" (I Peter 1:8). Many believers have governed their lives by this poem of wisdom:

> Only one life, 'twill soon be past,
> Only what's done for Christ will last.

QUESTIONS FOR DISCUSSION

1. Why do many ministers experience mental and emotional breakdowns? Can anything be done to prevent them from happening?

2. How are some ministers or sects handling the Word of God deceitfully today? What are some contemporary examples of religious dishonesty and craftiness?

3. How does Satan blind the minds of people today? Have his methods changed over the years?

4. How can a person preach himself? What would you do if your pastor did this?

5. Why are Christians afraid to witness to their neighbors? at work? at school? What can be done to encourage them?

6. How can faith healing be justified when the body is perishing every day? Are some Christians more interested in the strength of the body than in the strength of the soul?

7. Can Christians be so heavenly minded that they are no earthly good?

5

The Motivation for the Ministry

II Corinthians 5

Why do some Christians move toward spiritual maturity whereas others are content to remain in a carnal, immature condition? Why don't more Christians experience the abundant life (John 10:10)? Why don't all believers "press toward the mark for the prize of the high calling of God in Christ Jesus" (Phil. 3:14)? The answer is *motivation.* Some have it, but many do not. Paul was highly motivated. He "labored more abundantly" than others (I Cor. 15:10). In this chapter, he elaborates on three major doctrinal concepts that stirred him to great spiritual achievements.

I. THE IMMORTAL BODY (5:1–8)

Paul had just discussed his victory over the weakness of his present body, which he described as an "earthen vessel" (4:7), "mortal flesh" (4:11), and the "outward man" (4:16). He knew what he had done in spite of his physical limitations. Now he looked forward to what he could do for God in an immortal, incorruptible body with no such restrictions.

A. His Assurance of the New Body (5:1)

The conjunction "for" *(gar)* connects the doctrinal teaching of both chapters. One of the eternal, invisible things that he viewed is now discussed at length (cf. 4:18).

1. The end of the old body (5:1a)

The old body is described in two ways. *First,* it is an "earthly house." God has designed human life to function within a body suitable for living here upon earth.[1] A redeemed human being will not be able to use his present earthly house in the celestial holy city. The Corinthians were informed earlier that "flesh and blood cannot inherit the kingdom of God; neither doth corruption inherit incorruption" (I Cor. 15:50).

Second, it is a "tabernacle." The word "skin" is based upon the Greek word translated as "tabernacle" *(skēnos).* The present body is viewed as a temporary, portable tent that is erected for this life but taken down at death. Peter sensed that he would put off his tabernacle (that he would die) shortly after he wrote his second epistle (II Peter 1:13–14). God became man and pitched His tent among men (John 1:14).[2]

Paul realized that his present physical existence could not continue forever. He knew that his body would be "dissolved," but he did not know when.[3] It could come either through death or translation at the coming of Christ. John expressed the same hope: ". . . it doth not yet appear what we shall be: but we know that, when he shall appear, we shall be like him; for we shall see him as he is" (I John 3:2).[4]

1. The word "earthly" is a compound Greek word *(epigeios)* literally meaning "upon earth."

2. The word "dwelt" is the same as "tabernacled."

3. The usage of "if" *(ean* with the subjunctive) reveals the uncertainty of time, not of fact.

4. The phrase "when he shall appear" literally is translated "if he should be manifested." John did not doubt the fact of Christ's return; only the time was uncertain.

2. The beginning of the new body (5:1b)

The verb "have" shows the assurance of a present possession. He knew that the end of the old body did not terminate his personal existence. The new body would be part of the "inheritance incorruptible, and undefiled, and that fadeth not away, reserved in heaven" for all believers (I Peter 1:4). Paul knew that he would obtain a new body, but he did not know when. He describes his new body in five ways.

First, it is a "building" *(oikodomē).*[5] It is permanent and solid whereas the earthly body is temporary and fragile. *Second,* it comes from God ("of God"). The present body comes from human parentage, but God is the source

5. Tasker identifies the building with the mansions that Jesus is preparing (John 14:2). R.V.G. Tasker, *The Second Epistle of Paul to the Corinthians,* Tyndale New Testament Commentaries (Grand Rapids: Wm. B. Eerdmans Publishing Co., 1960), p. 78.

Athens, the cultural center of pre-Christian Greece, is nestled around the 512-foot-high hill known as the Acropolis (left). The temple structure dominates the summit.

of the new body. *Third,* it is "not made with hands." Jesus referred to His resurrection body in these terms (Mark 14:58). *Fourth,* it is "eternal" in that it will never wear out. It will never have to be changed. *Fifth,* it is a body designed for life "in the heavens." The believer's future is life eternal in the holy city (Rev. 21–22), not in this present universe, which will be destroyed by fire (II Peter 3:10–12).

B. His Desire for the New Body (5:2–5)

The verb "groan" is used twice to indicate the intense desire for the new body (5:2, 4). Paul's body ached in anticipation for it. All creation, in fact, groans for deliverance from the effects of sin (Rom. 8:19–23).

1. He wanted to be clothed (5:2)

Two metaphors (clothing and house) are used to describe the new physical manifestation of the self. To Paul, the future life would be far better than the present (Phil. 1:21–23). He wanted his heavenly house.

The verb "clothed upon" is a double compound *(ependuō* using three words *epi, en, duō).* It actually means to put one piece of clothing over another which is presently being worn. The usage in this context probably means that Paul wanted to be alive when the Lord returned. In that way, the new body could be put on right over the old one. Earlier, Paul did say: ". . . we shall be changed. For this corruptible must put on incorruption, and this mortal must put on immortality" (I Cor. 15:52–53).

2. He did not want to be naked (5:3)

If a person is alive on earth when Christ returns, he will go from one form of bodily existence to another. The self, clothed with the old body, will suddenly be clothed with the new, eternal body. If a believer dies before Christ's advent, the body will disintegrate and the immaterial self will go into the presence of Christ within the third heaven. He then will have to wait for the day of resurrection before he gets his new body, his eternal clothing. This period between the physical death of a believer and his resurrection is designated as the time of nakedness. It is when the self has neither its old body or its new body. Theologians have called it the intermediate state of the soul.[6]

This period of nakedness when the self has no bodily clothing is not to be feared by the child of God. Actually, in such a state, he is much better off than in his mortal body (Phil. 1:21–23). Nonetheless, the state in which the self is clothed with the eternal body is much better than the intermediate state. Thus, Paul desired the return of the Lord over the prospect of physical death.

3. He wanted life (5:4)

Paul's "tabernacle" was wearing out. His body groaned with physical pain; it was a weighty burden to him. There was much he could not do because of his weak frame. These difficulties, however, did not create a "death wish" within him. He enjoyed life, but he knew that life would be better in the eternal state.

He did not want to die simply to put off the old body with its infirmities. He did not welcome death as an escape. He did not desire the "unclothed" intermediate state. Rather, he wanted to be "clothed upon" with the new body. This could only happen if Christ returned in his lifetime. This was his intense desire. He wanted his mortal

6. Philip E. Hughes, *Paul's Second Epistle to the Corinthians,* New International Commentary on the New Testament (Grand Rapids: Wm. B. Eerdmans Publishing Co., 1962), p. 285.

state to be "swallowed up" by the immortal state. He wrote formerly: "So when this corruptible shall have put on incorruption, and this mortal shall have put on immortality, then shall be brought to pass the saying that is written, Death is swallowed up in victory" (I Cor. 15:54).

4. He wanted God's provision (5:5)

He was assured that God would give him the new body, whether through death and resurrection or through direct translation at Christ's return. There were two guarantees: God's purpose and His pledge.

God had purposed this goal for both the apostle and all believers. He "hath wrought us for the selfsame thing." God always completes His works (Phil. 1:6). He works in our lives "both to will and to do of his good pleasure" (Phil. 2:13).

God's pledge is in the giving of "the earnest of the Spirit" (5:56; cf. 1:22). The indwelling presence of the Holy Spirit within the believer's body is a divine guarantee that the Christian will get a new body. He stated elsewhere: "And not only they, but ourselves also, which have the firstfruits of the Spirit, even we ourselves groan within ourselves, waiting for the adoption, to wit, the redemption of our body" (Rom. 8:23).

C. His Desire for the Lord's Presence (5:6–8)

Beyond the deliverance from the infirmities of the mortal body, the apostle wanted to be in the presence of Jesus Christ. Again, this could be achieved through one of two ways: by death or by the return of Christ. The anticipated joy of seeing the Savior took precedence and preeminence over his own personal relief.

1. His absence (5:6)

Jesus Christ is both divine and human. Since He is God, He can be present everywhere in the totality of His divine being. He promised His disciples that He would be with them always (Matt. 28:20). Where two or three believers are gathered together in His name, there He is in the midst of them (Matt. 18:20). Every Christian is personally indwelt by the divine Christ (Gal. 2:20; Col. 1:27). In His resurrected human body, however, He is in the third heaven at the right hand of the Father (Heb. 1:3).

Paul knew that as long as he remained on earth in his mortal body he would be absent from the resurrected body of the Lord.

2. His walk (5:7)

The walk of the believer on earth is "by faith, not by sight." Paul looked with the eyes of faith "at the things which are not seen" (4:18; cf. Heb. 11:1). He had confidence that he possessed a new body although he had never seen it. Although Christ had directly revealed Himself to Paul on several occasions, he spent the bulk of his ministry without physical observation of the resurrected Christ.

3. His desire (5:8)

His confidence (emotional courage) and strong will overcame any fear of death, which most people have. He believed that Christ had "abolished death, and hath brought life and immortality to light through the gospel" (II Tim. 1:10). He knew that his death could be a means of glorifying Christ (Phil. 1:20). He often said: ". . . to die is gain . . . . For I am in a strait betwixt two, having a desire to depart, and to be with Christ; which is far better" (Phil. 1:21, 23).

Thus, Paul wanted to leave his life on earth ("absent from the body") for life in heaven ("present with the Lord"). He wanted to be home where he belonged.[7] His citizenship, his inheritance, and his Savior were all in heaven, so why should he not be there also (Phil. 3:20; I Peter 1:4)? There was no attraction on earth strong enough to weaken his desire to be with Christ. He practiced his own counsel: "If ye then be risen with Christ, seek those things which are above, where Christ sitteth on the right hand of God" (Col. 3:1).

II. THE JUDGMENT SEAT OF CHRIST (5:9–13)

All stewards of the mysteries of God must one day give an account of the discharge of their responsibilities (I Cor. 4:1–2). The faithful servant will not be afraid of that day, but the slothful servant will worry that he finally will be found out. Accountability is a necessary motivation in any vocation. It is more so in matters that pertain to God and to the souls of men.

A. His Ambition to Be Pleasing (5:9)

The connective "wherefore" joins the two sections. Also the mention of "present or absent" shows the continuity between the contrast of the two bodies and the divine evaluation of the personal self in either state.

1. His effort (5:9a)

The verb "labor" comes from a Greek word that literally means "to love honor" *(philotimeomai).* It means to act from a love of honor or to be ambitious in the good

7. The Greek word for "present" *(endēmeō)* means to be with your own people whereas the Greek word for "absent" *(ekdēmeō)* means to be away from your own people.

sense. Paul said that he "strived (same Greek word) to preach the gospel, not where Christ was named" (Rom. 15:20). He told the brethren to "study (same Greek word) to be quiet, and to do your own business" (I Thess. 4:11). When a redeemed sinner perceives all that God has done for him and all that he is in Christ, then he will live and serve out of love for honor. He will want to honor his God and the name of Christ that he bears.

2. His goal (5:9b)

The words "may be accepted" are literally "to be well pleasing."[8] There are levels of Christian living and service. John set forth these conditions for answered prayer: "And whatsoever we ask, we receive of him, because we keep his commandments, and do those things that are pleasing in his sight" (I John 3:22). Obedience is the duty of each Christian, but pleasing God involves something more.[9] Paul wanted to serve at this higher level. His ambition was to *be* well pleasing *(euarestoi),* not just to *do* pleasing things *(arestoi).* He went beyond conduct to character. Also, the addition of the adverb "well" enlarged the scope of his goal.

He wanted to be well pleasing to Christ ("him"). He once wrote: "For do I now persuade men or God? or do I seek to please men? for if I yet pleased men, I should not be the servant of Christ" (Gal. 1:10). This goal was constant. Both in his present experience and in his future presence before Christ, he wanted to please Christ.

8. The Greek *euarestoi einai* uses the adjective "well pleasing" in the emphatic position before the infinitive "to be."

9. The son takes out the garbage (obedience in his household chore), but then he decides on his own to wash out the garbage can (pleasing).

B. His Appearance to Be Judged (5:10)

The judgment of the believer was introduced in the first epistle: both future judgment (I Cor. 3:13–15; 4:1–5) and present judgment (I Cor. 11:28–32). The future aspect is emphasized here.

1. Nature of the judgment (5:10a)

Seven features are delineated. *First,* it is a necessity ("must," *dei*). A Christian *may* serve, but he *must* be judged. It is not optional, but obligatory.

Second, "all" believers will be judged. No one is exempt. Paul expected to be there (note his inclusion in "we"). Both the spiritual and the carnal, both the mature and immature, and both the clergy and the laity will be there. It is a judgment of the entire body of Christ.

Third, the judgment, however, will be individual. It is not a corporate judgment *per se;* rather each believer will be evaluated separately. Note how he switched from the plural ("we") to the singular ("everyone" and "he").

Fourth, it is a judgment of practice, not of position. Men are not here to find out whether they are saved; they are at this special judgment because they are saved. The unsaved will be judged later at the Great White Throne (Rev. 20:11–15). This is a judgment of the works done by the Christian in his present body ("according to that he hath done").

Fifth, the judgment will be conducted by Christ as He sits on "the judgment seat" *(bēma).* This word refers to a raised platform from which orations and legal judgments were given. In Roman times, every major city (including Corinth) had one from which political officials disseminated justice: Pilate in Jerusalem (Matt. 27:19; John 19:13); Herod Agrippa I at Caeserea (Acts 12:21); Gallio at Corinth (Acts 18:12, 16, 17); Festus at Caeserea (Acts

The surviving ruins of the Bema at Corinth. Here, Paul appeared before Gallio.

25:6, 17); and Caesar at Rome (Acts 25:10). All believers, however, will be judged at the *bēma* in heaven (5:10; cf. Rom. 14:10).

Sixth, the believer will "appear" at that time. This does not mean that he will simply put in an appearance; rather, he will literally "be manifested" *(phanerōthēnai).* He will be turned inside out. In that day, Christ "will bring to light the hidden things of darkness, and will make manifest (same word) the counsels of the hearts" (I Cor. 4:5). He will be revealed for what he really is. God, who looks on the heart, will show what the heart of each believer is really like (cf. Heb. 4:13).

Seventh, the judgment will occur immediately after the coming of Christ for believers. This passage emphasizes only the fact, and not the time, of the evaluation. Earlier, Paul wrote: "Therefore judge nothing before the time, until the Lord come . . . (I Cor. 4:5). Thus, this is not an ongoing judgment that each Christian experiences on earth or right after death. It is a once-for-all event that occurs right after the appearing of Christ (I Thess. 4:13–18).

2. Results of the judgment (5:10b)

First, the quality of the believer's practice will be shown to be either "good or bad." A good work manifests the character and will of God. Emphasis is on quality rather than quantity (cf. I Cor. 3:13; "what sort it is" not "how much it is"). It is permanent and valuable work (cf. I Cor. 3:12; "gold, silver, precious stones"). On the other hand, the "bad" work is a worthless, temporary effort done out of a selfish motivation (cf. I Cor. 3:12; "wood, hay, stubble").

Second, each believer will "receive" a reward for genuine spiritual work (I Cor. 3:14). These rewards are also called crowns: an incorruptible crown for living the disciplined life (I Cor. 9:25); a crown of rejoicing for witnessing (I Thess. 2:19); a crown of righteousness for loving Christ's appearing (II Tim. 4:8); a crown of life for enduring trials (James 1:12); and a crown of glory for faithful pastors (I Peter 5:4).

C. His Ministry to Be Manifested (5:11–13)

The conjunction "therefore" connects Paul's projected future manifestation of his ministry before Christ with his proposed present manifestation before the church. A proper understanding of the future will affect present behavior.

1. He persuaded men (5:11)

Paul knew "the terror of the Lord." He had a holy awe and reverence for the sovereign Christ. He did not view his ministry as optional or something that could be performed with effort less than his best. He confessed: ". . . for necessity is laid upon me; yea, woe is unto me, if I preach not the gospel!" (I Cor. 9:16). Believers should express their Christian life "with fear and trembling" (Phil 2:12). G.Campbell Morgan asserted that once we had fear that He would hurt us, but now we should fear lest we hurt him. [10]

He persuaded men by telling them exactly what God wanted them to hear. He testified to both Jews and Gentiles that Jesus Christ was God manifest in the flesh and that He died and was resurrected according to the divine redemptive plan (Acts 18:4; 28:23).

He knew that God had already examined his life and ministry and that he had been approved ("we are made manifest."). It was now his hope that his entire ministry would be manifested within their "consciences" so that they would evaluate him as God had already done. He had nothing to hide from either God or man.

2. He did not commend himself (5:12–13)

Paul did not want to brag about his spiritual achievements to win the loyalty and admiration of the Corinthians (5:12a; cf. 3:1). The members of the church who embraced the apostle's authority and example did it without much specific knowledge of his private life. To help this group to have a logical, factual defense of his authority, Paul decided to reveal some important data about himself (5:12b). The false teachers were only interested in achievements that could be objectively itemized ("glory in appearance"). They were not impressed by internal qualities ("not in heart"). Paul decided that his supporters should defend him on common ground with the false teachers.

10. G. Campbell Morgan, *The Corinthian Letters of Paul,* (Westwood, N.J.: Fleming H. Revell Co., 1956), p. 242.

Paul was aware that even his self-disclosures would be misunderstood (5:13). Some would think that he was insane ("beside ourselves").[11] But the friends of Jesus thought that He was "beside himself" (Mark 3:21; same word). After hearing the apostle, the Roman procurator Festus loudly charged: "Paul, thou art beside thyself; much learning doth make thee mad" (Acts 26:24). Regardless, the apostle claimed that he was doing it in the interest of God.[12] On the other hand, some might think that Paul was "sober," or right minded in what he revealed about himself. If so, then he had done it for their benefit. To the accusation of Festus, Paul replied: "I am not mad . . . but speak forth the words of truth and soberness" (Acts 26:25).

III. THE WORK OF GOD (5:14–21)

All believers should be motivated constantly by what God has done for them. Paul was. At his conversion on the road to Damascus, he said, "Lord, what wilt thou have me to do?" (Acts 9:6). He then spent his entire life doing the will of God.

A. Christ Loved Him (5:14–15)

1. Christ's love for Paul (5:14)

How clear are the words: "For the love of Christ constraineth us." The verb "constraineth" literally means "to hold together" *(sunechō).* Christ used it of Himself: "But I have a baptism to be baptized with; and how am I strait-

11. The phrase "beside ourselves" ("ecstasy") is based upon this Greek word *(exestēmen).* Robertson sees this as a criticism of Paul's tongue speaking and visions. A. T. Robertson, *Word Pictures in the New Testament,* 6 vols. (Nashville: Broadman Press, 1931), 4:230.

12. Both phrases "to God" and "for your cause" are Greek datives of interest.

ened (same word) till it be accomplished" (Luke 12:50). Christ did not fall apart as He approached the cross. So it was with Paul. The love of Christ held him together so that he could finish his tasks regardless of what men were doing to him.

But was it Christ's love for Paul or Paul's love for Christ that formed the constraining force?[13] Both, of course, were true, but the former is what overwhelmed the apostle and caused him to respond with loving obedience. Christ loved us so much that He died in our place ("for all"). He was our substitute, bearing our sin and penalty on the cross. He "was delivered for our offences, and was raised again for our justification" (Rom. 4:25). Later, he wrote:

> For when we were yet without strength, in due time Christ died for the ungodly.
>
> For scarcely for a righteous man will one die: yet peradventure for a good man some would even dare to die.
>
> But God commendeth his love toward us, in that, while we were yet sinners, Christ died for us (Rom. 5:6–8).

Paul knew that he deserved hell, but Christ gave him heaven. He never got over the joy of that realization.

2. Paul's life for Christ (5:15)

The unsaved man is "dead in trespasses and sins" (Eph. 2:1). When he appropriates by faith the value of Christ's atonement, he then becomes mystically identified with the Savior in His death and resurrection. He has died with Christ and he has been raised with Christ ("then were all dead," literally, "then all died"). Just as death no longer has dominion over the risen Christ, so sin no longer has dominion over the redeemed sinner (Rom. 6:1–11; Gal. 2:20; Eph. 2:4–6).

13. The words "of Christ" grammatically can be either subjective genitive (Christ loved Paul) or objective genitive (Paul loved Christ).

This identification should manifest itself in the experiences of the believers. They "should not henceforth live unto themselves, but unto him which died for them and rose again" (5:15). Such redeeming love should be reciprocated with altruistic service, not with selfish gratification. Acceptance of justification should lead to a desire for sanctification.

B. God Made Him into a New Creation (5:16–17)

This truth is a result of Christ's love for him. The logical connection is seen by the double usage of *hōste,* translated both as "wherefore" (5:16) and "therefore" (5:17).

1. His knowledge was new (5:16)

As the result of his conversion, Paul no longer viewed men as the unsaved world evaluated them ("after the flesh"). He was no respecter of persons. He was not impressed with race, social strata, financial status, physical appearance, or native abilities. He once had gloried "in appearance," but he now repudiated that method of evaluation (5:12).

He no longer viewed Christ as he once did in his unregenerate state.[14] In his spiritual blindness, he measured Christ outwardly. He hated Him and persecuted His followers.

He "now" wanted to see men as God sees men. He saw them as needy sinners for whom Christ died. He saw all believers as one in Christ (Gal. 3:28). He was impressed with what God had done in and through the lives of men. He was interested in the "heart" (5:12).

14. Some have concluded on the basis of this verse that Paul may have seen Christ during the Lord's earthly ministry. But Paul does not clearly make that statement.

2. His position was new (5:17)

Four truths are set forth. *First,* he was "in Christ." Throughout his epistles, Paul stressed that the believer is accepted by God because he is in Christ (Eph. 1:3, 4, 6). Christ affirmed this truth: ". . . ye shall know that I am in my Father, and *ye in me,* and I in you" (John 14:20).

Second, he was a "new creature." This is true both of the believer's position (Gal. 6:15) and practice (Eph. 2:10). He is a member of the "new man," the body of Christ composed of both saved Jews and Gentiles (Eph. 2:15). This position is gained through the baptism in the Holy Spirit (I Cor. 12:13).

Third, his past spiritual position has "passed away." The "old things" do not refer to past sinful habits; rather, they point to the reasons why a sinner stands condemned before a holy God.[15] It is not true that all old sinful practices vanish at conversion. Many Christians bring into their new life some of their old sinful habits and attitudes. The New Testament contains corrections of such vices.

Fourth, his new position before God was permanent and complete.[16] The phrase "all things" refers to the believer's unalterable standing before God, not to his behavior of life.[17]

C. God Reconciled Him (5:18–20)

Three key doctrinal words summarize the nature of the atonement. The idea behind *redemption* is the purchase

15. Consult the author's book *Salvation Is Forever* (Moody Press, 1974), Chapter One: "What does it mean to be lost?"

16. The verb "are become" is in the Greek perfect tense *(gegone).* This shows a permanent state which is the result of the past conversion act.

17. Again, consult the author's book *Salvation Is Forever,* Chapter Two: "What does it mean to be saved?"

price necessary to redeem man from his position under sin (Rom. 3:24). The death of Christ provided the *propitiation* that satisfied the righteous justice of God (Rom. 3:25; I John 2:2). The purpose behind *reconciliation* was to remove the barrier of sin so that sinful man could return to God (5:18).

1. Reconciliation of Paul (5:18)

The phrase "all things" connects the two sections (5:17; cf. 5:18). The new spiritual position has been made possible by God ("of God") who has done two things. *First,* He reconciled Paul. This is an accomplished fact, provided at the cross and appropriated at conversion ("hath reconciled"). The object is "us." Reconciliation provided is not the same as reconciliation accomplished. Although Christ died for all men, all men are not saved because they have not believed. Also, only sinful man needs reconciliation. God did no wrong, therefore He has no error to admit. God did not walk away from man, but man walked away from God. God's goal is to bring men back "to Himself." The means is "by Jesus Christ." Man cannot set the terms of reconciliation; he must accept or reject the gracious terms laid down through the death of Christ.

Second, God gave to Paul "the ministry of reconciliation." It is within God's good pleasure that reconciled sinners inform unreconciled sinners that the way back to God has been made available.

2. Reconciliation of the world (5:19)

The ministry of reconciliation has a threefold nature.[18] *First,* Paul preached that "God was in Christ reconciling the world unto himself." All men can return to God be-

18. The words "reconciling," "imputing," and "committed" are all participles.

cause Christ died for all men. They must, however, come in God's way and under his terms (John 3:16; 14:6).

Second, in reconciliation, God does not hold the sins of the sinner against him. He has removed the sin barrier. Through each sin, man kept closing another door after him as he went farther away from God. In reconciliation, God has opened up all of the doors. It is now up to the sinner to return.

Third, Paul looked upon himself as one who should take "the word of reconciliation" to others. Sinners must be told that they can return if they want to.

3. Reconciliation of the church (5:20)

Because God had entrusted to him the ministry of reconciliation, Paul saw himself as an "ambassador."[19] He was the envoy of God to man, bearing a vital message. An ambassador does not speak in his own name, does not act on his own authority, and does not declare his own opinions. Rather, he is a representative of the country that sent him. Paul used three phrases to convey that political metaphor: "for Christ," "God did beseech you by us," and "in Christ's stead."

To whom was the command given ("be ye reconciled")? It may have been stated to the unbelieving element within the church. But it seems more plausible that Paul was addressing genuine Christians. They had already experienced spiritual reconciliation to God at their conversion. Now Paul wants them to be reconciled to God as dissident believers by accepting him as God's representative. Thus, this is reconciliation within the family structure.

19. The word "ambassador" comes from a basic Greek word *presbus,* meaning "old man" and later used of a political or religious representative.

D. God Made Him Righteous (5:21)

1. Imputation of sin to Christ (5:21a)

Reconciliation and forgiveness are possible because God "made [Christ] to be sin for us." The Savior was not made a *sinner* on the Cross; rather, he was made *sin* (singular). Isaiah wrote that Jehovah "hath laid on him the iniquity of us all" (Isa. 53:6). He took away "the sin of the world" (John 1:29). God imputed or reckoned to Christ human sin. When that occurred, the wrath of God fell upon Him. He bore both the sin and the penalty for that sin.

In His divine-human person, He "knew no sin." Only He could say: "Which of you convinceth me of sin?" (John 8:46). He was "without sin" (Heb. 4:16) and "separate from sinners" (Heb. 7:26). He "did no sin" (I Peter 2:22). John stated that "in him is no sin" (I John 3:5). And yet he died, "the just for the unjust, that he might bring us to God" (I Peter 3:18).

2. Imputation of righteousness to us (5:21b)

When a sinner believes in Christ, his sin is forever forgiven and he is "made the righteousness of God in him." In Christ ("in him"), the believer is clothed with the righteousness of God (I Cor. 1:30). God sees the repentant sinner in His Son and declares him to be righteous.

QUESTIONS FOR DISCUSSION

1. Why do Christians fear death when they know that they will be in the presence of God? What can be done to prepare believers for death?

2. What are examples of walking by faith and walking by sight? Can they ever be synonymous?

3. What are some specific examples of good and bad works? Why do men and God view Christian effort differently?

4. In what ways do believers glory in appearance? How can the situation be corrected?

5. Why do most Christians lack motivation? Why do they have to be threatened or begged to do something for the cause of Christ?

6. Did Christ die for all men? Or did He die only for those He intended to save? Should either view minimize evangelistic zeal?

7. What are some of the new things that belong to every Christian?

6

The Purity of the Ministry

II Corinthians 6:1—7:1

Who ministers to the minister? In most cases, he has to minister to himself. The apostle said to his young associate Timothy: "Take heed unto thyself, and unto the doctrine; continue in them: for in doing this thou shalt both save thyself, and them that hear thee" (I Tim. 4:16). If a minister fails to minister to himself before he ministers to others, he has failed. He must *be* before he can *do*. The familiar charge to the physician to heal himself can be applied: "Minister, minister to thyself!"

In the discharge of his service, Paul was careful to watch out for his own life. In this chapter, he pointed out two areas that manifested the purity of his ministry.

I. LACK OF OFFENCE (6:1–10)

Paul had charged in the first epistle: "Give none offence, neither to the Jews, nor to the Gentiles, nor to the church of God" (I Cor. 10:32). The word "offence" *(proskopē)* literally means "to strike against." When a person strikes his foot against a projection on a path, he may trip or stumble. No believer should be like that projection. He should not cause a saved or an unsaved person to stumble through his disobedient life. Paul had determined never to be an offence (I Cor. 8:13).

A. In His Appeal to the Church (6:1–2)

1. Basis of the appeal (6:1a, 2)

Paul had to say to the Corinthian Christians what needed to be said, but he wanted the tone of his approach to be inoffensive. In his appeal for them to be reconciled to God and to himself (5:20; 6:11–13; 7:2), he wanted them to respond positively. To do so, he followed a fourfold procedure.

First, they were co-workers.[1] Believers should complement each other rather than compete against one another. They should make their distinctive contributions to the work of God, but they should all have the common goal to glorify Him (I Cor. 3:5–8). They are "laborers together with God" (I Cor. 3:9). They should work out what God is working in their lives (Phil. 2:12–13). God especially works with His own people. Thus, a believer cannot be a co-worker with God if he chooses to cooperate with false teachers.

Second, he expressed his concern over their spiritual condition with his appeal ("we beseech," *parakaleō).* He did not use an abrasive command; rather he used a gentle technique, "even as a nurse cherisheth her children" (I Thess. 2:7).

Third, he equated his concern with that of God ("for he saith"). This Old Testament quotation comes from a context in which God will give help to His servant in the day when salvation is offered to the Gentiles (Isa. 49:8).

Fourth, the double usage of "now" shows the urgency of the time. Reconciliation should never be delayed. Paul wanted them to be reconciled to God and to himself immediately. Just as God held nothing against them, so

1. The word "synergism" comes from the Greek word translated as "workers together" *(sunergeō).*

Paul did not view their past mistreatment of him as a barrier to their future friendship. The immediate context (5:18–6:2), which deals with the nature of salvation, may indicate that Paul viewed some of the members of the church to be unsaved. Their hostility toward the apostle may indicate a lack of reconciliation toward God. The suggestion that they might be spiritual reprobates will be made later (13:5).

2. Purpose of the appeal (6:1b)

He did not want them to receive "the grace of God in vain." This goal could have a double application. *First,* it could refer to believers who have an acceptable standing before God but who will only have bad works to display at the judgment seat of Christ (5:10; cf. I Cor. 3:15). *Second,* it could refer to unsaved members of the Corinthian church who knew the facts of the gospel but who had never believed personally in Christ. Or, it could refer to those who thought that to be saved they needed to add circumcision and legalism to their Christian profession. Earlier, the apostle had criticized the vain faith of denying the resurrection of the body (I Cor. 15:2). False teaching had made its inroads into the church, and Paul was fearful that some had succumbed to its influence. If he did not warn them, then he would have actually offended them.

B. In His Ministry Before God (6:3–4a)

In his apostolic ministry, the apostle had two major goals: one negative and one positive. They are indicated by the usage of two participles: "giving" and "approving."[2] Thus, they show that in his horizontal appeals to other

2. Grammatically, these participles must be joined to the verb "we beseech."

men, he never forgot who he was in his vertical relationship to God.

1. Giving no offence (6:3)

He was absolutely emphatic in his resolution not to offend.[3] Regardless of circumstances ("in any thing"), he did not want to cause anyone to stumble just once ("no," literally "not one").

To Paul, "the ministry" was greater than himself. That *it* not be blamed, *he* had to be blameless. The concept behind "blame" is that of mocking and ridicule. The name "Momus" was assigned to the pagan god of ridicule.[4] The apostle did not want the world to ridicule the nature of the ministry because of his failures. Thus he strived not to fail. The concepts of "blots" or "blemishes" *(mōmos)* are also related to the essence of blame. He did not want to scar the ministry nor did he want to handle it with dirty hands.

2. Approving himself (6:4a)

He did not believe in commending himself to others (3:1; 5:12), but he did aspire to commend himself before God.[5] No man can fool God. Paul knew that; thus he wanted to serve faithfully. As a prisoner before the Roman governor Felix, he testified about himself: "and herein do I exercise myself, to have always a conscience void of offence toward God, and toward men" (Acts 24:16). If a man's life is right before God, it will be right before men.

3. The emphatic Greek double negative is found here. Literally, it reads "giving not one offence in not one thing."

4. The Greek word for "blame," *mōmeō,* is related to this pagan name.

5. The Greek word for "approving" is the same as that for "commending."

Since God had put him into the ministry, Paul had no private life. He was a minister first and foremost. To him, it was a great privilege and an awesome responsibility. There is no greater vocation. Thus, he wanted his life to manifest those qualities that should characterize the glory of the gospel ministry.

C. In His Behavior in the World (6:4b–10)

As life is unpredictable, so also is behavior. Most people permit circumstances of life to control their emotional responses. But genuine Christian character, developed and controlled by the Holy Spirit, will dictate one's behavior regardless of the circumstances. It is easy to rejoice when things are going well, but it is difficult to sing when times are hard. Paul wanted his life and ministry to be free of offence in all situations.

Earlier, mention was made of "in any thing" and "in all things" (6:3–4). Now, these general phrases are broken down into four major categories with further specific listings.[6] In the passage, they are indicated by the words "in" *(en),* "by" *(dia),* and "as" *(hōs).* A. T. Robertson observed: "Each word in the listing carries a story that can be filled in from Paul's own life as a preacher with an echo in that of us all."[7]

1. In outward difficulties (6:4b–5)

Ten words are listed within prepositional phrases, all beginning with "in" *(en).* They could be seen as parallel. They seem, however, to fall into three groups of three

6. Grammatically, there probably are only three categories, but the first one has been arbitrarily divided for outline purposes.

7. A. T. Robertson, *Word Pictures in the New Testament,* 6 vols. (Nashville: Broadman Press, 1931), 4:234.

words each. These three groups in turn describe "patience." Paul patiently endured for Christ. He remained free of offence in spite of all the pressures and problems heaped upon him.[8]

The *first* group of words deals with those trials into which God brought him. The word "afflictions" *(thlipsesin)* includes all experiences in which pressure was placed upon him (Acts 14:22; 20:23; Rom. 8:35). Jesus predicted that all believers would go through these tribulations (John 16:33). Paul earlier described the comfort of God that came to him in those hours of trouble (1:4; same word). The word "necessities" *(anagkais)* refers to the financial and physical hardships that result from such difficult trials (I Thess. 3:7; translated as "distress"). The concept of "distresses" *(stenochōriais)* means those situations where there is no room to turn around. In modern culture, it points out those times when all four walls seem to be closing in. It usually produces frustration and depression (cf. 4:8). Paul, however, followed the counsel of the Psalmist: "I called upon the Lord in distress: the Lord answered me, and set me in a large place " (Ps. 118:5; cf. I Cor. 10:13).

The *second* group of words refers to those hardships inflicted upon Paul by sinful men. The word "stripes" *(plēgais)* naturally includes all of the beatings that the apostle experienced, either by whip or rod (11:24–25; cf. Acts 16:23, 33). He had bled and endured excrutiating pain. He could honestly say: ". . . I bear in my body the marks of the Lord Jesus" (Gal. 6:17). In many cities he had to undergo "imprisonments" where he was illegally mistreated (11:23). The "tumults" point to the riots caused by unbelieving Jews and pagans who aggressively

8. The word "patience" literally means "to remain under" *(hupomenō).*

opposed his preaching (Acts 13:50; 14:19; 16:19; 19:29; 21:30). The word literally means "not according to stability" *(akatastasiais).* Wherever the apostle went, both revivals and riots exploded.

The *third* group of words points to those hardships that Paul willingly imposed upon himself. The concept behind "labours" *(kopois)* is fatigue created by strenuous effort. He became bone weary in his spiritual ministry, in traveling much of the time, and in the physical work of making tents. The word "watchings" refers to those times of sleeplessness, when he went to bed late and got up early or when he could not sleep because of the pain in his body (11:27; II Thess. 3:8). The term "fastings" includes those times when he deliberately went without eating to finish some aspect of his ministry.

2. In spiritual response (6:6–7a)

In many ways, the times of difficulty molded Paul's character. They provided occasions in which his inner man could be strengthened and manifested. As adverse winds threatened to blow him over, he sank his spiritual roots deeper into God. He could say, whether in sunshine or in shadow: "Ye are witnesses, and God also, how holily and justly and unblameably we behaved ourselves among you that believe" (I Thess. 2:10).

His life was marked by "pureness," a moral cleanness of person and of purpose.[9] Although he admitted his deficiencies in pulpit oratory, he knew that he had "knowledge" (11:6). This refers to spiritual wisdom divinely imparted and taught by the Holy Spirit (I Cor. 2:12–13; II Peter 3:15). He manifested "longsuffering" toward

9. All of the phrases in this section introduced by the word "by" are actually begun with the preposition "in" *(en),* the same as in the preceding section.

those who aggravated and opposed him (I Cor. 13:4). The basic meaning of "longsuffering" *(makrothumia)* is to put anger or wrath far away from oneself. His "kindness" could be seen in his good deeds toward those who irritated him (I Cor. 13:4). He overcame evil with good. Kindness is grace in action (Luke 6:35).

These marvelous spiritual qualities were not the result of moral reformation, but "by the Holy Spirit." The apostle was so yielded that the Spirit produced an abundant crop of spiritual fruit through his life (Gal. 5:22–23). He thus manifested a "love unfeigned." His love was genuine, not hypocritical (Rom. 12:9; I Peter 1:22). He loved both his enemies and friends (Matt. 5:44). He did not compromise "the word of truth" when times were difficult. He upheld and spoke it. He continued to preach it in the face of opposition (Eph. 1:13; Col. 1:5). He knew that it was the only solution for man's sin (James 1:18). He endured and ministered as "the power of God" enabled him. It was such divine power that wrought salvation in his listeners and deliverance for himself (I Thess. 1:5).

3. Through conflict (6:7b–8a)

Paul had just declared how he inwardly responded to his outward difficulties. Now, in a threefold series, he pointed out the conflict that he endured to gain the victory.[10]

He used "the armor of righteousness" (cf. Rom. 6:13). It was "the armor of light" (Rom. 13:12). It was the armor of God composed of the girdle of truth, the breastplate of righteousness, the gospel shoes of peace, the shield of faith, the helmet of salvation, and the sword of the Spirit (Eph. 6:10–17). These weapons could repel Satanic attacks either from the right side or the left. The weapons

10. All three phrases are introduced by the preposition *dia*, translated as "by."

"on the right hand" are offensive weapons whereas those "on the left hand" are defensive.

He had an approved ministry "by honor and dishonor" (literally, "through glory and dishonor"). There were times when men praised his ministry, and there were occasions when men misrepresented Paul's efforts. In either situation, he remained adamant in his determination not to give offence. In any house, there are vessels of honor and vessels of dishonor (II Tim. 2:20). Unfortunately, men falsely identified Paul as a vessel of dishonor. He knew nevertheless that he possessed the treasure of God within his earthen body (4:7). Paul desired the honor of God more than the praise of men (John 5:44; 12:43).

He endured through "evil report and good report." Some spoke the truth about him, but others lied or bore false witness. Although it would be easy to react carnally in such situations, the apostle did not. Christ loved and forgave those who crucified Him, and Paul loved those who assassinated his character.

4. In misrepresentation (6:8b–10)

Throughout his life, Paul fought innuendo and false charges. In this section, he admitted that he appeared to be one thing, but in reality, he was just the opposite. He recognized that some reported false data about him completely contrary to the real facts. Others were constantly offending him, but he resolved not to offend them in turn. He isolated seven such false reports. They seem to fall into three major areas.

The *first* group of two contrasts deals with his *reputation.* His critics claimed that Paul and his associates were "deceivers," but actually they were "true" witnesses. The English word "planet" is based upon the Greek word for "deceivers" *(planoi).* They claimed that Paul was a wandering impostor. In actuality, the critics were the real deceivers. The false teachers also charged that Paul was "unknown" in Palestine as a real leader of Christianity (cf. Gal. 1:22–23). Some Jewish leaders said that they had never heard of him (cf. Acts 28:21–22). The apostle knew, however, that he was well known to God and to the spiritually minded (John 10:14; II Tim. 2:19). He definitely was known by the Corinthian church (11:6).

The *second* group of three contrasts deals with his *health.* Since Paul was at the point of death many times, many had reported that his life and ministry were finished ("dying"). But it was just at those times that Paul would begin a new project with increased vitality ("we live"). He earlier admitted that the deterioration of his body simply caused his spirit to become stronger (4:16). Increasing age and physical weakness did not slow him down. Many viewed Paul's hardships as the discipline of God for secret sins. His critics were like Job's comforters. Paul knew that his tribulations would not destroy him, but rather he would learn more qualities of spiritual sonship through his chastening (cf. Heb. 12:3–11). Some charged him to be "sorrowful," but the seriousness of his spiritual determination did not remove his inner spirit of "rejoicing" (Phil. 4:4).

The *third* group of two contrasts deals with his *finances.* His critics deprecated Paul's manual labor and simple life style. They claimed that his lack of money revealed a lack of divine blessing upon his life. Although he was poor financially, he was still able to make "many rich" spiritually. Christ said that the church at Smyrna was poor, yet rich, and that the church at Laodicea was rich, yet poor (Rev. 2:8–11; 3:14–19). Spiritual wealth is infinitely more valuable than material riches. Peter and John could not give any money to the lame beggar, but they did give him both physical and spiritual wholeness (Acts 3:6). Paul, at the end of his life, possessed only a cloak, some books, and a few friends (II Tim. 4:9–13), but he was an heir of the world (I Cor. 3:21–23; Gal. 4:7). Solomon wrote: "There is that maketh himself rich, yet hath nothing: there is that maketh himself poor, yet hath great riches" (Prov. 13:7). The critics were in the first group, but Paul was in the second.

II. SEPARATION (6:11–7:1)

To be "a vessel unto honor, sanctified, and meet for the master's use, and prepared unto every good work," a believer must separate himself from sin and from false teachers (II Tim. 2:19–22). To be sanctified means to be set apart or to be separate from. The purity of the ministry demands the purity of the minister.

A. Their Separation From Him (6:11–13)

Loved ones, however, should not be separate from each other. If disagreements should separate them temporarily, they should seek reconciliation immediately.

1. Paul wanted them back (6:11–12)

In four concise statements, he expressed concern over their separation from him and their lack of separation from sin and false teachers. The insertion of the vocative, "O ye Corinthians," intensified his emotional appeal for their repentance (cf. Gal. 3:1).

First, he said that "our mouth is open unto you." He had just revealed innermost thoughts about himself and his relationships to them and to God. He had confessed everything. He did not speak with "tongue in cheek."

Second, his "heart was enlarged." His heart was big enough to include them even with their indifference and rebellion. He later said that "ye are in our hearts to die and live with you" (7:3). As in the marriage vows, he loved them for better and for worse. The more he appealed to them, the more his love increased for them. He subsequently admitted: "And I will very gladly spend and be spent for you; though the more abundantly I love you, the less I be loved" (12:15). Christ said that the heart expresses itself in speech (Matt. 12:34), and Paul had just done that. God gave to Solomon a "largeness of heart" (I Kings 4:29), and the apostle had received the same.

Third, he stated: "Ye are not straitened in us." To be straitened means to be restricted, to be crowded, cramped, or confined. In his active life and absence from their city, Paul had not crowded them out of his life.

Fourth, they actually had shut him out of their lives ("ye are straitened in your own bowels"). His critics had caused them to narrow their place for him in their hearts. They had room for questions and suspicions about him. The more they did that, the more their love and loyalty diminished.

2. Paul wanted them to want him back (6:13)

Paul desired an equality and a reciprocity in their relationships. Just as the unsaved will receive a "recompense of their error" (Rom. 1:27), a judgment suitable to their rejection of God, so Paul wanted them to respond with attitudes and actions suitable to his treatment of them. He wanted "a recompense in the same."

He manifested the heart and the speech of a loving father (I Cor. 4:15). He now wanted them to show the heart and the speech of loving children.

His heart was enlarged, but theirs was restricted. He then issued the command: "Be ye also enlarged." Paul lamented that his spiritual children did not love or want him. He urged them to open their hearts to him.

B. Their Need for Separation From Error (6:14, 17)

Real separation involves separation *from* as well as separation *to.* In their conversion, the Thessalonians "turned *to* God *from* idols" (I Thess. 1:9). Thus, to return to Paul, they would have to turn away from their alliances with error. In the marriage ceremony, a man vows to separate himself from other women to be joined to one. Throughout married life, the husband must keep that commitment. Such commitment applies also to spiritual relationships.

The apostle's call for separation can be seen in four direct commands.

1. Be ye not unequally yoked together with unbelievers (6:14a)

The imperative literally reads: "Stop becoming unequally yoked" *(mē ginesthe heterozugountes).*[11] Some had already violated the principle. They were yoked with the unsaved in voluntary marriage, in violations of Christian liberty (I Cor. 10:16–22), in toleration of unsaved church members, and in support of the false teachers. The apostle wanted these practices to stop.

The principle behind the unequal yoke is based upon the Old Testament law: "Thou shalt not plow with an ox and an ass together" (Deut. 22:10). There was to be separation in the breeding of animals, the planting of crops, and the usage of sewing materials in clothing (Lev. 19:19;

11. It is the present middle imperative of *ginomai,* deponent, used with the negative. It means to stop doing what you are already doing.

Deut. 22:9–11). Thus, the program of God for the church cannot be carried out by the union of Christians with the unsaved. God's work must be done only by God's people and in His way.

2. Come out from among them (6:17a)

The next three commands are based upon the principle behind the admonition of God to Israel ("saith the Lord"): "Depart ye, depart ye, go ye out from thence, touch no unclean thing; go ye out of the midst of her; be ye clean, that bear the vessels of the Lord" (Isa. 52:11). Just as the Levitical priests had to separate themselves from the idolatrous priests, so the Corinthians had to come out from their associations with the Judaizers or with the pagan temple banquets.

The command was decisive.[12] There was to be no delay. It had to be done immediately and totally.

The apostle John issued a similar command for believers to withdraw from Babylon: "Come out of her, my people, that ye be not partakers of her sins, and that ye receive not of her plagues" (Rev. 18:4). The lack of separation will produce sin and judgment for believers in this life.

3. Be ye separate (6:17b)

There cannot be separation within unequal associations. Separation is basically positive, toward God, but it can only take place after departing from sin and unholy alliances. The order of these commands verifies that conclusion.

The concept behind "be separate" *(aphoristhēte)* is to mark off boundaries beyond which you will not go. These

12. The imperative is in the aorist tense: *exelthete.*

fences of restriction must be based upon obedience to the revealed truth of Scripture.

4. Touch not the unclean (6:17c)

The command literally reads: "Stop touching anyone or anything which is characterized by uncleanness."[13] Once the distinctive position of separation has been established, there should never be a contact with any unequal association again.

C. The Argument for Separation (6:14–18)

This section begins and ends with commands. The support for the commands is indicated by the first usage of the connective "for" (6:14; *gar*). Three lines of argument are followed.

1. It is biblical and logical (6:14b–16a)

In a series of five questions, Paul demonstrated that the union of the saved with the unsaved is unequal and illogical. *First,* there is no "fellowship" between righteousness and unrighteousness (literally, "lawlessness," *anomia*). The word for "fellowship" *(metochē)* means to have with or to share with. These patterns of behavior are mutually incompatible.

Second, there is no "communion" *(koinōnia)* between light and darkness. These two have nothing in common. They cannot coexist. Jesus said: "I am the light of the world; he that followeth me shall not walk in darkness, but shall have the light of life" (John 8:12). God is pure, moral

13. *akathartou mē aptesthe.* This is the present imperative with the negative. It means to stop doing what you are doing. The adjective "unclean" is in the emphatic first position in the sentence. It can be either masculine (person) or neuter (thing) in word gender.

light. There is not a single speck of darkness within His being (I John 1:5). Therefore, to have fellowship with Him, one must walk in the light and not in the darkness (I John 1:6).

Three, there is no "concord" between Christ and Belial (6:15a). The English word "symphony" comes from the Greek word for "concord" *(sumphōnēsis).* The name "Belial" comes from a Hebrew word meaning "worthlessness" and is ascribed to the person of Satan. It is unthinkable that Christ and Satan would harmonize in a duet or that they would work together in a common project.

Four, there is no "part" between a believer and an unbeliever ("infidel," literally "a not believing one, *apistou).* They have no common standing before God, nor do they have a common eternity facing them.

Fifth, there is no "agreement" between the temple of God and idols. The presence of idols within the Jewish tabernacle or temple was absolutely forbidden. The inner sanctuary, or the Holy of Holies ("temple," *naos),* was God's exclusive dwelling place. It was not to be polluted by the erection of idols within it. The meaning of "agreement" is "to place down with" *(sugkatathesis).* The ark of the covenant with the mercy seat was not to be placed beside a heathen idol.

2. The sanctity of believers (6:16)

In the Old Testament economy, God manifested His presence in the tabernacle constructed by Moses, the temple built by Solomon, and the second temple rebuilt by Zerubbabel (Lev. 26:11–12; Ezek. 37:27). In the New Testament era, however, He manifests His presence in the lives of believers.

Christians today are "the temple of the living God." He dwells within the body of each believer (I Cor. 6:19–20).

The local church corporately is also the temple of God (I Cor. 3:16–17). God walks among them. He is their God, and they are His redeemed people.

Because God has set Christians apart to be His sanctuary, they then should sanctify their lives for holy purposes. If they enter into alliances with the unsaved, they involve God and violate the sanctity of their bodies. When Israel went into apostasy, they usually erected idols within the temple (II Kings 21:7; 23:6–7; Ezek. 6:3–18). When revival broke out, the idols were removed and the sanctuary was cleansed. It must be so also in the life of each Christian.

3. The blessings of obedience (6:17b–18)

Two are mentioned. *First,* God will "receive" the obedient, separated child of God. This is not a reception to salvation, but to full enjoyment of the privileges of sonship. In their relationship to God, Paul wanted the Father to receive them, but in their personal relationships to him, Paul wanted them to receive him (7:2). The second would logically follow the first if obedience were practiced.

Second, there would be an awareness of the Father–Son relationship (6:18). It was difficult for the prodigal son to sense his sonship when he was living far away from his father, indulging in riotous living and, later, working in the pig fields (Luke 15:11–24). When he repented and returned home, the Father kissed, forgave, clothed, and fed him. So it will be for any Christian who will separate himself from sin and sinful alliances.

D. His Commitment to Holiness (7:1)

The connective "therefore" joins the two chapters (6 and 7) and forms the conclusion to the present section on separation.

1. The Command

Just as the Jewish temple had to be cleansed of its idolatrous pollution, so Paul exhorted: "Let us cleanse ourselves from all filthiness of the flesh and spirit." He included himself ("let us").[14] It was to be done thoroughly and immediately. No uncleanness was to remain.[15] It was a self-cleansing event ("ourselves"). Each believer was to deal with his own sin. It also dealt with the sins of both the flesh and the spirit, both of the body and of the mind.

Cleansing follows forgiveness and reconciliation. A child who became dirty by playing in the mud must still be washed after he has been forgiven by his mother.

14. This is a hortatory subjunctive, a command issued both to the speaker himself and to his listeners. It is also in the aorist tense. It was to be a decisive, once-for-all event.

15. The words "cleanse" and "unclean" come from the same Greek root.

The southeast corner of the temple area at Jerusalem.

2. The basis of the command

The possession of the promises of blessing should stimulate each Christian to live a separated life ("having therefore these promises"). No believer gives up anything to have the blessing of living in the will of God. It is the disobedient Christian who loses out.

The usage of the vocative "dearly beloved" shows that Paul loved them regardless of their inferior behavior. He wanted his love to motivate their decision to obey.

3. The goal of the command

It is not enough to get rid of sinful practice. It must be replaced by an aggressive determination to be holy. Paul wanted them to perfect "holiness in the fear of God" (cf. Phil. 2:12–13; Heb. 12:14). This is a life-long process and struggle.[16]

16. The participle "perfecting" is in the present tense.

QUESTIONS FOR DISCUSSION

1. In what ways can people receive the grace of God in vain? Can anything be done to prevent it?

2. How can the ministry be blamed? Cite some specific, contemporary illustrations.

3. Are the lives of modern Christians and ministers different than those of Paul's day? Is this good or bad?

4. How can Christians have two different evaluations of the same minister? How can this cause confusion in the life of a church?

5. Why do parents and children sometimes fail to love each other equally? What about the love between the pastor and his people?

6. Why do some Christians refuse to separate themselves from sinful associations?

7. To what extent should the principle of separation be carried? What about business partnerships, marriages, denominational affiliations, or city-wide evangelistic campaigns?

7

The Cares of the Ministry

II Corinthians 7:2-16

Throughout his ministry, Paul encountered both opposition and persecution from the unsaved. On top of that pressure was "the care of all the churches" (11:28). He had loving concern for all his spiritual children (Phil. 2:20). He was concerned more about the needs of others than about his own (Phil. 2:4).

I. HIS CONCERN (7:2–12)

In this passage, he expressed his concern over the Corinthians in three areas. It demonstrated that he was not a cold, heartless person; rather he was tender and extremely sensitive. He was compassionate, like the father of the prodigal son (Luke 15:20).

A. Their Reception of Him (7:2–4)

He was concerned whether the church would accept him. He began with an emotional appeal: "Receive us." The verb "receive" means to make room for *(chōrēsate)*.[1] They had forced him into a small corner of their hearts

1. This is a different word for "receive" than in 6:17.

(6:12–13). He wanted them to make more room for him in their hearts.

1. He gave them no cause for rejection (7:2)

Earlier, he said that he had given no offence in anything (6:3). Now, he claimed that he had scripturally offended "no man."[2] For a man under attack, this was a bold assertion. Three denials are enumerated. *First,* he "wronged" no man. He did no injustice *(ēdikēsamen).* He could honestly say that he was "pure from the blood of all men" (Acts 20:26). He knew that his methods were "not of deceit, nor of uncleanness, nor in guile" (I Thess. 2:3).

Second, he "corrupted" no man. Men were no worse off because of their contact with the apostle and his ministry; rather they were better. He ruined no lives. He could warn them not to defile or to corrupt the local church because he himself had never done this (I Cor. 6:17).

Third, he "defrauded" no man. He did not take advantage of anyone, although he was in a position to do so. He did not exploit their rebellion (cf. 2:11). He was not after their money or praise.

2. He held nothing against them (7:3)

When a marriage weakens, it is easy for each partner to blame the other. But Paul did not do this. He did not mention the conflicts, their lack of response, and his innocence "to condemn" them. He both forgave and forgot. He did not want to make them feel bad over and over because of what they did to him.

For example, when a man approaches marriage, he should realize that there will be both good and bad times.

2. The word translated as "no man" is emphatic in all three instances, occurring at the beginning of each phrase.

He takes the woman for better or for worse. Paul manifested that type of love. He made that commitment. The Corinthians were in his heart "to die and live" with them (7:3b).

3. He boasted about them (7:4)

When hard times enter a marriage relationship, it becomes too easy to forget the good times. The apostle did not. He remembered, though they had forgotten. When personal relationships become strained, it is better "to accentuate the positive and eliminate the negative." Paul boasted of four positive areas within his relationship to them.

First, he could speak frankly and openly to them ("great is my boldness of speech toward you"). Some people close their ears when disagreements arise. They give the silent treatment to others. The barriers of communication are broken down. Fortunately, Paul could still talk to them, send representatives to them, and write to them. At least they were willing to listen to what he had to say.

Second, he could glory in what God had done in their lives in the past and what He was doing for them in the present. He could speak of these good things to others. He did not criticize them before others. He kept their mutual differences to himself.

Third, they had given him "comfort" on many occasions. The most recent gift of their encouragement came through the glowing report of Titus (7:7).

Fourth, they had given him joy in the midst of his tribulation. The two verbs "I am filled" and "I am exceeding joyful" show his great delight over them. His cup was running over. No matter what happened to him, he could always thank God for them (I Cor. 1:4).

B. Their Reception of Titus (7:5–7)

Paul was concerned whether the church would receive Titus and accept his ministry. Before Paul left Ephesus for Greece, he had sent Titus to Corinth to prepare his way. Since the situation was tense, the apostle wondered what would happen.

Both Paul and Titus had agreed that they would meet in Troas if at all possible (2:12–13). When Titus did not come, however, Paul became apprehensive and moved into Macedonia.

Actually this passage (7:5–16) continues the narrative broken off earlier with a description of the gospel ministry (cf. 2:12–13).

1. He had no rest (7:5)

The anxiety at Troas was intensified when Paul came into Macedonia, the northern province of Greece. Here were the key cities of Philippi, Thessalonica, and Berea.

He flatly admitted that his "flesh had no rest." Earlier, he claimed that he had no rest in his spirit when Titus failed to appear at Troas (2:13). The usage of "flesh" and "spirit" here are synonymous. It shows that his concern permeated his entire life experience and his total being. This was no vacation trip for his physical and psychological relaxation.

He was "troubled on every side." The burdens and cares of the ministry pressed upon him from all directions. *First,* "without were fightings" refers to the persecutions from the unsaved. When the apostle was in Macedonia, on his second missionary journey, he was beaten and imprisoned at Philippi by the pagans and the city government officials, hassled at Thessalonica by the unbelieving Jews, and forced out of Berea by those same Jews (Acts 16:12–17:14). This present trip into Macedonia, therefore,

Ruins at Philippi, the chief city of Macedonia, where Paul established a Christian colony.

was the first time that he had revisited the area (7:5). The same forces opposed him.

Second, in addition, "within were fears." This was an intimate admission to make. After all, he wrote that "God hath not given us the spirit of fear; but of power, and of love, and of a sound mind" (II Tim. 1:7). In this confession, he revealed that he was a man with feet of clay; that he "was a man subject to like passions as we are" (James 5:17). These fears were not just for his own concerns, however, but they were also over the absence and safety of Titus. He was worried about his associate and could not understand why he had not come.

2. He was comforted by the coming of Titus (7:6)

The connective "nevertheless" (literally, "but," *alla*) sounds a note of triumph. What encouragement these two words can bring to the needy sinner or to the depressed saint: *But God!* (cf. Eph. 2:4).

He identified God as the one "that comforteth those that are cast down." Earlier, he called Him "the God of all comfort" and described His comforting ministry at length (1:3–11). The usage of the present tense ("comforteth") shows that divine encouragement is available at every moment of every day.

It is accessible, however, only for "those that are cast down." This refers to those who have been humbled *(tapeinous)*. When the circumstances of life have put a man on his back, he has only one place to look: up into the face of God. James said that tribulations are designed to make men low so that they later can be raised by God (James 1:9–10). Humility is prerequisite to exaltation (James 4:10; I Peter 5:5–6). In those times, the believer must learn to cast all his care upon God (I Peter 5:7).

Comfort, which has its source in God, often has human means. In this instance, it came "by the coming of Titus." The mere sight of his friend gave Paul joy and consolation. In times of distress, the appearance of friends can buoy the anxious spirit. In the first epistle, the apostle acknowledged his joy at "the coming of Stephanus and Fortunatus and Achaicus," the church messengers (I Cor. 16–17). At the end of his life, Paul wanted to be surrounded by such friends as Luke, Timothy, and Mark (II Tim. 4:9–11).

3. He was comforted by the report of Titus (7:7)

The appearance of Titus, in itself, was sufficient to give the apostle comfort and joy. The addition of the adverb "only," however, shows that Paul got more than he expected. Even if Titus had brought a bad report about the spiritual condition of the church, he would have felt joy because of the safety of his friend. What excited him further was the nature of the report. It was all good.

God comforted Paul through the comfort that Titus had received from the Corinthians ("by the consolation wherewith he was comforted in you"). It is a joy to see others comforted. Titus had left Paul for Corinth with some apprehensions himself (7:15). He was, however, well received. When the revival broke out, the church comforted the associate even more. The good feeling within Titus warmed Paul's heart as well.

Titus then reported that the Corinthians had deep concern over Paul in three areas. *First,* they had an "earnest desire" to see the apostle. He had changed his travel plans twice because he believed that they did not want to see him (1:15–2:1). *Second,* they were in "mourning" over all of the grief they had caused for the apostle. They were deeply sorry for their carnal rebellion. *Third,* they had a "fervent mind" (literally "zeal," *zēlos*) to defend him against his remaining critics. They were ready to stand for him and with him.

Paul reacted to this positive report: ". . . so that I rejoiced the more." What God had done in their lives was humanly unimaginable. It epitomized his prayer of confidence: "Now unto him that is able to do exceeding abundantly above all that we ask or think, according to the power that worketh in us . . ." (Eph. 3:20).

C. Their Reaction to His Letter (7:8–12)

He was concerned over what they would think and what they would do when they read his letter. Although some Bible students have equated this letter with I Corinthians, it is more plausible to see it as one just carried to the church by Titus. He referred to this epistle earlier: "For out of much affliction and anguish of heart I wrote unto you with many tears" (2:4). His inner fears at Troas and at Macedonia were caused to some extent by the severe emotional tone of his correspondence.

1. He was concerned when he wrote the letter (7:8)

At the time he wrote the painful letter, he wondered whether he had done the right thing. When Titus left Paul with the letter, the apostle wished that he could have recalled or rewritten it ("though I did repent").[3] Emotionally he had some misgivings or regrets. Did he say the right things in the right way? Did he say too much, or too little? These nagging questions contributed to his persistent anxiety over the situation.

But he had no misgivings when he heard what the letter had accomplished ("I do not repent"). The epistle achieved its intended purpose, and for that reason he was thankful.[4] He knew that God had sovereignly controlled both the writing and the reading of the letter. God had marvelously used the letter to produce godly sorrow within the lives of the Corinthians.

The sorrow was both personal and corporate (double usage of "you," plural). It was also temporary ("though it were but for a season"). If sorrow continues indefinitely, the grieved person could become very depressed (cf. 2:7). Sorrow must be replaced by positive attitudes and behavior. The word for "season" is literally "hour" *(hōra),* a

3. The Greek word translated as "repent" *(metamelomai)* is different from the typical word translated as "repent" *(metanoeō).* The first emphasizes a change of feeling whereas the second stresses a change of mind.

4. The Greek word for "letter" is *epistolē*, transliterated as "epistle."

term used for a very short period of time (cf. I Thess. 2:17).

2. He was concerned over the nature of their sorrow (7:9–10)

After Titus further explained the character of their sorrow and repentance, Paul could say: "Now I rejoice." No one is happy when he has caused someone else to be unhappy. Such a person would be sadistic. He wanted them to know that he did not rejoice just because "they were made sorry." That, in itself, did not give him any delight.

He did rejoice that they "sorrowed to repentance." Sorrow in itself is not repentance, although many equate the two. The goal of genuine sorrow should be repentance.[5] This word for "repentance" is *metainoia,* meaning a change of mind and behavior. This is the type of repentance necessary for genuine conversion (Matt. 4:17; Acts 26:20). It is also required for genuine reconciliation within the family of God. Their grief over their sin and mistreatment of Paul caused them to change their attitude toward him and to send Titus back to him with their apologies.

He rejoiced that their sorrow was "after a godly manner." It was literally "according to God" *(kata theon).* Their sorrow and repentance were according to a divine standard, not a human one. God produced the change in their lives; Paul did not.

He rejoiced because their repentance eliminated any further need for him to discipline them with apostolic authority ("that ye might receive damage by us in nothing"). He had indicated beforehand that he did not want to come with the rod of chastisement or in heaviness (2:1; cf. I Cor. 4:21). He could now come for their gain rather than their loss.

5. The goal is indicated by the preposition "to" *(eis).*

Sorrow works changes within a person. Like a catalyst, it produces results, either good or bad. It all depends on whether it is a godly or a worldly sorrow.[6]

First, "godly sorrow worketh repentance *(metanoian)* to salvation not to be repented of *(ametamelēton).*" There are two different words for repentance in this verse. A godly sorrow will produce a genuine change of mind and behavior, which will result in salvation. There will be no regrets over the desire to be saved or to be reconciled. A real Christian should not feel sorry that he is a Christian, and a repentant backslider will not feel sorry that he has been restored to fellowship. No believer should feel sorry that God has worked in his life.

Second, "the sorrow of the world worketh death." Many unsaved people out of remorse commit suicide or withdraw from their loved ones and responsibilities. Judas, who betrayed Christ, "repented himself" (Matt. 27:3; *metamelētheis).* He had regrets over what he had done, and he could not face himself or Christ. He returned the thirty pieces of silver and confessed to the priests: "I have sinned in that I have betrayed the innocent blood" (Matt. 27:4). His confession, however, should have been before God. Instead of praying to God or going to the apostles, he went out and hanged himself (Matt. 27:5). His sorrow was of the world. Judas was an unsaved man expressing remorse in a natural manner.

But Paul was glad that the sorrow of the Corinthians could be classified in the first category.

6. There is a parallelism in the literary construction. The first is literally "the according to God sorrow" *(hē kata theon lupē),* whereas the second is "the of the world sorrow" *(hē tou kosmou lupē).*

3. He was concerned over the nature of their repentance (7:11)

Genuine repentance is permanent as well as observable. A temporary reformation is a sign of human change rather than divine. Peter warned against those professed believers who "are again entangled therein, and overcome" with the pollutions of the world (II Peter 2:20). Paul was concerned whether their repentance was genuine or false. The report of Titus proved that it was genuine. The apostle then acknowledged it: "For behold this selfsame thing, that ye sorrowed after a godly sort." He then praised them for the characteristics of genuine repentance, which Titus had observed and reported to him. Real sorrow "worketh" real repentance (7:10), and theirs had "wrought" a real change in their attitudes.[7] They definitely were working out what God was doing in their lives (Phil. 2:12–13).

The *first* characteristic was "carefulness." It literally means "diligence" *(spoudē).*[8] A genuinely repentant person will quickly attempt to secure reconciliation with the person whom he has offended and to make immediate restitution. He will not delay. The same word describes a Christian as "not slothful *(spoudē)* in business" (Rom. 12:11).

The *second* was "clearing of yourselves." It is based upon a Greek word *(apologia),* transliterated as "apology." It ordinarily means a logical defense of one's beliefs and practices (cf. Acts 22:1; I Peter 3:15). They did not justify their rebellion, but rather, they supported their repentance with real proofs.

7. These two verbs "worketh" and "wrought" are from the same Greek word *katergazomai.*

8. The English word "speed" is the transliteration of it.

The *third* was "indignation." This refers to their recognition of the shame that their behavior had brought upon them. They blushed with red faces. They reacted like the publican, who "standing afar off, would not lift up so much as his eyes unto heaven, but smote upon his breast" (Luke 18:13).

The *fourth* was "fear." They realized that they had sinned against a holy God and His apostolic representative. They then sensed the judgment that they could have received. That awareness gave them fear over what might have been.

The *fifth* was "vehement desire" (same word as "earnest desire," 7:7). Some people, in their shame and sorrow, do not want to see the people against whom they have sinned. In real repentance, the offender must face the offended. He will want to see them to set things right.

The *sixth* was "zeal" (same word as "fervent mind," 7:7). The offender should want the offended party to feel better. He will desire the honor of that person. He will not contemplate just his own feelings, but he will seek the benefit of the offended party.

The *seventh* was "revenge." They possessed a willingness to be punished. They knew that they deserved it. Within the church, there was also a desire to discipline the sinning parties.

In conclusion, Paul applauded them: "In all things ye have approved yourselves to be clear in this matter."[9] The word "clear" *(agnous)* indicates that they were pure and guiltless in their procedure of repentance. They told everything. They did everything they had to do. They did not hide anything. It was all out in the open. For this, all could rejoice.

9. The Greek word for "approved" is the same as that for "commended" (3:1; 5:12).

4. He was concerned over their understanding of him (7:12)

Paul wondered whether they would perceive the real purpose for writing the painful letter. He had hoped that they would not take it negatively, but positively.

His negative concerns were twofold. *First,* he did not aim the letter at the one who "had done the wrong" (cf. 2:2, 5–6). He was not trying to get back at this critic. His motivation was not vendetta or a desire for personal revenge. This approach would be contrary to his spiritual convictions (Rom. 12:17–21). *Second,* he did not write the letter to support the cause of the one who "suffered wrong." Although this could be an impersonal reference to himself, it probably refers to a supporter of Paul within the church.[10] He did not "choose up sides."

He wrote, rather, out of a positive concern: ". . . that our care for you in the sight of God might appear unto you." He did it to show his love for them (2:4). The word "appear" is again the word "to be manifested inside out" (cf. 5:10–11). In that painful letter, they saw his tears and bleeding heart (2:4). He wept for them because he could not bear to see what they were doing to themselves. At the risk of further alienation, he had to take drastic action. Now that the tensions had been removed, he could explain the full intent behind the letter.

II. HIS COMFORT (7:13–16)

This section of the epistle ends as it began: with the joy of comfort (cf. 1:3–11). Comfort comes through both God and people.

10. If there was no lost letter, then it could refer to the two defendants in the legal dispute (I Cor. 6:1–8).

A. From Titus (7:13–15)

1. The joy of Titus (7:13)

After their sorrowful repentance, the church was comforted by the ministry of Titus and by the communication of Paul's feelings through Titus. Their encouragement then supported the apostle's own comfort ("Therefore we were comforted in your comfort").[11] Real comfort is reciprocal. For example, sometimes a patient in the hospital bed ends up comforting the visitors.

The joy of Titus gave the apostle more joy ("exceedingly the more joyed we for the joy of Titus." Happiness is contagious. Titus was beaming when he arrived in Macedonia to rejoin Paul.

Titus stood exhilarated before Paul ("his spirit was refreshed by you all").[12] The joy of seeing the Corinthians change before his very eyes had not left the associate's memory. It was ever fresh. The exuberance of Titus gave Paul further assurance that the church had experienced genuine repentance.

2. The boast of Paul (7:14)

Paul revealed to Titus everything that he knew about the church before Titus left on his mission. In fact, the apostle had boasted about their good qualities to the associate. He pointed out the problems, but he also spoke highly of them (cf. I Cor. 1:4). He was not "ashamed" that he had done so. Sometimes, it is not good to talk about personal differences with a third party, but Titus was trustworthy.

11. The word "in" is *epi,* which normally means "upon." Paul's comfort was on top of theirs.

12. The verb "refreshed" is perfect *anapepautai.*

Whether in person or by epistle, Paul spoke the truth to the Corinthians. Thus, his boasting to Titus was also true. His boasting literally "became truth" before Titus' very eyes at Corinth.[13] What Paul said and what happened matched completely. The apostle probably told Titus what to expect from them if a revival broke out, and, sure enough, it happened.

3. The love of Titus (7:15)

This was the first direct encounter of Titus with the Corinthian church. He doubtless had some reluctance, because both Timothy and Paul before him had failed to solve the complicated problems (2:1; I Cor. 4:17; 16:10–11). Paul had originally gone to the sophisticated city "in fear and in much trembling" (I Cor. 2:3). So it was natural for Titus to go with the same "fear and trembling" (7:15).

The church, however, prepared by the Spirit of God, "received him." They welcomed him. They then gave "obedience" to him by following the directives of Paul's epistle. When that occurred, the fear was converted into love ("inward affection"). He had compassionate concern for their spiritual well-being. He loved them dearly, and he hated to leave them. But he had to tell Paul the good news.

B. From the Church (7:16)

Paul could honestly say to them: "I rejoice therefore that I have confidence in you in all things." This verse serves as a fitting conclusion to the first seven chapters and is an appropriate transitional expectation for the content of the next six. He had "confidence" that they would yield to the ministry of Titus. Now he has confidence that

13. The phrase "is found a truth" comes from *alētheia egenēthē.*

they will complete the collection (chapters 8-9) and that they will excommunicate the false teachers (chapters 10-13).

QUESTIONS FOR DISCUSSION

1. Should pastors leave their churches at the first sign of dissension? Can pastors be wrong in their attitudes as well as the people?

2. Do believers encourage each other enough? What can be done to promote this practice?

3. In what situations are the presence of friends a comforting influence? Are there any times when Christians should be alone?

4. What present fightings and fears can mark the lives of believers? of ministers?

5. Can you recall any instances when you wished that you had not said or written something? Did it turn out well or badly?

6. Do we see real repentance taking place today? Where do shame and restitution fit in?

7. Do Christians often fail to do some good just because their intentions might be misjudged? Cite some illustrations. What can be done about it?

8

The Welfare Collection

II Corinthians 8

Giving is the essence of Christianity. God "so loved the world that he gave his only begotten Son" (John 3:16). The old English word "charity" was often used to translate the Greek word for "love" *(agapē)*. To give one's time or money can be love in action.

The early church believed in and practiced giving to the needy. The apostles used the treasury of the church at Jerusalem to distribute to "every man according as he had need" (Acts 4:35; 6:1–3). Later, in a time of famine, the church at Antioch sent relief through Paul and Barnabas to the believers at Jerusalem (Acts 11:27–30). Paul counseled: "As we have therefore opportunity, let us do good unto all men, especially unto them who are of the household of faith" (Gal. 6:10).

Near the end of his third missionary journey, Paul asked the churches of Galatia, Macedonia, and Achaia to give to a relief collection for the poor Christians in Jerusalem. He had already informed the church at Corinth about the procedure to follow (I Cor. 16:1–4), and they had willingly agreed to cooperate (8:10). At the time Paul wrote this epistle, he was in the process of gathering the collection. The money from Macedonia and probably that from

Galatia was in hand, but he had not yet received the Corinthian contribution. Thus in these next two chapters (8-9), he encouraged them to collect their share in the financial project before he arrived from Macedonia. Apparently they did (Rom. 15:25–28).

I. THE PRINCIPLES OF BIBLICAL GIVING (8:1–15)

Just as there is a difference between godly sorrow and the sorrow of the world (7:10), so there is one between mere philanthropy and biblical giving. The former stems from man to man whereas the latter should manifest the love of God through men to other men. The goals and motivations are radically different.

A. As Seen in the Macedonians (8:1–5)

Churches were established in the Macedonian cities of Phillipi, Thessalonica, and Berea during the apostle's second journey (Acts 16:12–17:14). They were founded just a few months before the church at Corinth was begun.

In their gift to the welfare collection, Paul recognized four principles of genuine biblical giving that he wanted to share with his readers.

1. It manifested the grace of God (8:1)

Their giving demonstrated what the grace of God can do in lives. The word "grace" is emphasized in this section, occurring seven times in this chapter and three times in the next. The essence of grace is to give, to give abundantly, to give abundantly to people whom you do not know, and to give with no expectation of anything in return. Christ said: "And if ye do good to them which do good to you, what [grace] have ye? for sinners also do even the same" (Luke 6:33).[1]

Most of the Macedonian Christians, in their unsaved days, were anti-Semitic (cf. Acts 16:20; I Thess. 1:9). When they were born again, however, they became one with the Jews in Christ. Their pagan hostility disappeared and now they demonstrated their love for the Jewish Christians in distant Jerusalem with a remarkable gift. Only the grace of God could have motivated that type of generosity.

2. It was liberal (8:2)

Their giving reflected "liberality" *(aplotētos).* Jesus used this word when He spoke about the difference between heavenly and earthly treasure: ". . . if therefore thine eye be single [same word], thy whole body shall be full of light" (Matt. 6:22). Liberal giving is done out of simplicity, or from a single-minded purpose to glorify God. It is uncalculating and free from ulterior motives.

Four aspects of their liberal giving are described. *First,* they gave "in a great trial of affliction." They themselves were in need. God was testing them in the fires of persecution, and they came out as refined steel.[2]

Second, their giving demonstrated the "abundance of their joy." The Thessalonians were converted "in much affliction with joy of the Holy Ghost" (I Thess. 1:6). Their joy over what God had given them in Christ caused them to give liberally. They had a joy over what they could give and over what they lost because of their faith. They were like the Hebrew Christians who "took joyfully the spoiling

1. The word translated as "thank" is really "grace" *(charis).*

2. The word "trial" *(dokimē)* was used of the testing of metals in fire.

of [their] goods, knowing in [themselves] that [they] have in heaven a better and an enduring substance" (Heb. 10:34).

Third, they gave out of "deep poverty." They were not just poor; some were *extremely* poor. Their regional natural resources had been exploited by the Romans. Through civil wars and persecution, they became even more impoverished. And yet, they gave like the poor widow who cast her two mites into the temple treasury. She "of her want did cast in all that she had, even all her living" (Mark 12:44). They both needed their gift money to pay for the daily necessities of life, but they loved God so much that they gave it to Him.

Fourth, their gift manifested their spiritual "riches." They were like the church at Smyrna, which was poor, yet rich (Rev. 2:9). They personified Solomon's wisdom: "There is that maketh himself poor, yet hath great riches" (Prov. 13:7).

3. It was voluntary (8:3–4)

Their giving was free, self-imposed. They were "willing of themselves" *(authairetoi)* to share. This concept literally means "self choosing." They did it out of their own initiative.

All believers can give something ("for to their power," literally, "according to ability"); but they exceeded their power to give. They went beyond the call of duty. They went beyond Paul's expectations of them.

In fact, they forced Paul to accept their gift. They first begged the apostle to let them participate, and then they begged him to take the money ("praying us with much intreaty that we would receive the gift"). Paul probably told them originally that they did not need to give since they were in financial need themselves. Now, he wanted them to take some of the money back, but they refused. The Macedonians responded to the need like the Israelites did when a call went out from Moses for materials to construct the tabernacle. So much came in that Moses had to stop them from giving any more (Exod. 36:5–7). Such giving is practically nonexistent today.

They wanted to share in "the fellowship of the ministering to the saints." They were fellow members of the family of God with the Jerusalem saints, so they wanted to share with their spiritual brothers.

4. It was to the Lord (8:5)

The quantity of the gift impressed the apostle, but the spiritual quality of the givers went beyond his expectations. God does not want the gift without the giver; He does not desire man's wealth apart from his will.

Their outward giving of money manifested the inward giving of "themselves to the Lord." They had done this "first." Vertical giving should precede horizontal giving. They followed Paul's admonition: "I beseech you therefore, brethren, by the mercies of God, that ye present your bodies a living sacrifice, holy, acceptable unto God, which is your reasonable service" (Rom. 12:1). Once a believer has yielded himself completely, he is then in a position to offer the sacrifices of money (Phil. 4:18) and of praise (Heb. 13:15–16).

They gave both themselves and their money to Paul, the representative of the Lord (8:5b). They acknowledged themselves to be obedient servants "by the will of God."

B. As Seen in the Corinthians (8:6–9)

Within these instructions given to the church, other principles of genuine biblical giving can be seen.

1. It was to be the completion of a goal (8:6)

Paul wanted the Corinthians to have the same experience in giving as the Macedonians. Although the church had begun a year before to set aside money (8:10), the process had sputtered and probably ceased, doubtless caused by all of the dissension within the church. When Titus was there, the giving started up again as the result of the revival ("as he had begun"). Thus, he "desired Titus" to return to Corinth to "finish" the collection project. He wanted God to perfect "the same grace" in them as He had done among the Macedonians. He desired that they would be marked by the same principles.

What God begins, He completes (Phil. 1:6; I Thess. 5:24). When a genuine work of divine grace occurs within a believer, it will lead to the completion of goals. In true revival, a person finishes what he starts out to do.

2. It is a grace gift (8:7)

The church at Corinth was a gifted church (I Cor. 12–14), but it was deficient in the gift of giving. Up to this point, they had not expressed themselves in the area of generosity. In the first epistle, he acknowledged their possession of the grace gifts *(charismata):* "So that ye come behind in no gift" (I Cor. 1:7). Now he wrote: "Therefore as ye abound in everything" (8:7a). The church had all of the necessary spiritual equipment for real success.

He isolated five areas in which the church had shown excellence. *First,* the gift of "faith" was a special faith to attempt great tasks for God (I Cor. 13:2). All Christians are justified by faith and should walk by faith, but this gift seems to be connected with outward demonstrations of divine power (cf. I Cor. 12:9–10; 13:2). *Second,* the gift of "utterance" *(logō;* literally "word") refers to prophecy and possibly includes tongues-speaking (I Cor. 14). *Third,* the gift of "knowledge" pointed to their understanding of revealed truth in both doctrinal and practical areas (I Cor. 12:8; 13:2). *Fourth,* the gift of "diligence" manifested their enthusiastic zeal to do the will of God. Thus, in what they believed, what they said, what they knew, and how they practiced it, they had no peers. *Fifth,* in spite of the disagreements, they still maintained a genuine love for Paul.

Paul wanted their giving to match their religious zeal: "see that ye abound in this grace also." The gift of giving was a grace gift imparted by the Spirit of God. It was so listed: "he that giveth, let him do it with simplicity" (Rom. 12:8).

3. It should demonstrate love (8:8)

Paul did not command them to give ("not by commandment"). Giving must not be forced or required; it must be a free expression of a person's grateful heart.

He wanted them to know what others had done. The phrase "the forwardness of others" refers to the intense enthusiastic zeal that the Macedonians had put into their giving.[3] Since the Corinthians were proud of their religious diligence, the apostle wanted them to see that others had surpassed them in this one area.

In the first epistle, he had criticized them for their lack of love in using their gifts (I Cor. 13). As the result of the revival, they had freshly renewed their love for each other, for Christ, and for Paul. Now, he wanted them "to prove the sincerity of [their] love" through their participation in the collection. The word "sincerity" *(gnēsion)* connotes

3. The words "diligence" and "forwardness" come from the same Greek word *spoudē.*

that which is legitimately born, not spurious.[4] Real love for the Father can be seen in real acts of love toward needy brethren (I John 3:17–18).

4. It should reflect Christ's giving (8:9)

All grace gifts should manifest "the grace of our Lord Jesus Christ." What He did should be seen in what we do. We should love, forgive, forbear, and give as He did (Eph. 5:2, 25; Col. 3:13). The Corinthians were knowledgeable beneficiaries of His sacrificial love and grace ("ye know"). Grace is "**G**od's **R**iches **A**t **C**hrist's **E**xpense." Giving is the very essence of grace.

Christ "was rich." He was and is God. Before His incarnation, He manifested and enjoyed the riches of His divine glory (Phil. 2:6). In the possession of righteousness, there was no one richer than He, and there was no one poorer than we. But Christ loved us, and when a person loves, he wants others to have what he has. He wants to give. Thus Christ "became poor" for our benefit ("for your sakes"). He became man, and then He became sin for us on the cross (5:21). At that time, spiritually speaking, there was no one poorer than He. Because of that loving act, all believing sinners become "rich." They possess the righteousness of God. In Christ, there are no people richer than Christians. He impoverished Himself that we might become wealthy. The Prince of peace became a pauper that we who are spiritual paupers might become princes. The conclusion is obvious: If Christ gave so much, should we not give also?

5. It should manifest willingness (8:10–12a)

It was "expedient" for them to finish what they had started (8:10–11a). It was necessary for the total develop-

4. It is based upon *ginomai* and *gennaō,* verbs which deal with birth.

ment of their spiritual character. Before any others had given, the Corinthians had voluntarily decided to participate and had actually started their fund ("who have begun before, not only to do, but also to be forward a year ago").[5] In their letter to Paul, they had asked him about proper procedures to follow in the accumulation of the money (I Cor. 7:1; 16:1–4). But during the year, very little money had been contributed.

Paul then charged them: "Now therefore perform the doing of it" (8:11a). This admonition came in the form of "advice" rather than as a stern "commandment" (8:10; cf. 8:8). They needed to do what they had willed to do.

Their giving had to be done out of a "willing mind."[6] Just as the noble Bereans received the Word of God with all "readiness of mind" (Acts 17:11), so they had to welcome joyfully the opportunity to share. Likewise, men should become pastors "not for filthy lucre, but of a ready mind" (I Peter 5:2). They originally started with a willing mind and now they should finish with the same willing mind.

6. It should be according to what one has (8:12b)

All believers should give, but all cannot give the same amount. God does not expect someone to give what he does not have. A believer, however, must prayerfully look at what he does have and then willingly give out of that resource. Certainly, the wealthy should give more because they have more. There is no indication in this passage that a definite percentage must be given. The percentage that a wealthy believer could give should be higher since he has more than the poor Christian both before and after giving.

5. The infinitive "to be forward" is literally "to will" *(thelein).*

6. Both "readiness" and "willing mind" come from the same Greek word *prothumia.*

However, the widow with her two mites gave a higher percentage of what she had than the Pharisees, although the amount of the gift was much smaller.

7. It should reveal equality (8:13–15)

In biblical giving, every one should give his fair share. The standard is "equality" *(isotētos)*.[7] Paul did not expect the wealthy Corinthians to give more than their fair share ("ye burdened"). He did not expect them to carry the load of giving that other churches should have done ("For I mean not that other men be eased"). The imagery is of two beasts of burden. Instead of both of them being laden with equal weight, more is placed on one than the other. One is "eased," whereas the other is "burdened."

At the same time, there is no equality between "abundance" and "want" (8:14). It is not right for those believers who have abundance of money to selfishly keep their money when they see their spiritual brothers who are in want. Out of their abundance they should give to meet the needs of those who lack. Paul firmly believed that the saints in Jerusalem would have given to the Corinthians if the financial roles had been reversed ("that their abundance also may be a supply for your want"). He, however, may have contrasted the financial wealth of the Corinthians with the spiritual wealth of the Jerusalem church. He later said:

> For it hath pleased them of Macedonia and Achaia to make a certain contribution for the poor saints which are at Jerusalem.
>
> It hath pleased them verily; and their debtors they are. For if the Gentiles have been made partakers of their spiritual things, their duty is also to minister unto them in carnal things (Rom. 15:26–27).

7. An *isoceles* triangle is one with two equal sides.

Paul wanted the provision of God to be equally distributed, regardless of who had been given the most (8:15). When God supplied manna to the Jewish nation in the wilderness, no one went hungry (Exod. 16–18). Those who were able to gather more than what they needed shared with the aged and infirmed. Needs were met daily. If anyone selfishly hoarded manna, it became spoiled overnight. The principle is clear. Some believers, because of geographical location, business timing, and ability, are able to make more money than others. They should look upon their profit as a stewardship from God, which they must share with the unfortunate in this life. If they selfishly lay up treasure on earth today, they will have no reward in the tomorrow of eternity (Matt. 6:19–21).

II. THE SENDING OF REPRESENTATIVES (8:16–24)

To prepare the church for his visit, Paul sent some of his associates to carry the letter, to consummate the collection, and to solidify his authority against the threat of the false teachers. Paul trusted his young associates and often sent them on difficult assignments.

A. Their Identification (8:16–22)

1. Titus (8:16–17)

Paul gave "thanks to God" that He had placed "the same earnest care into the heart of Titus" which He possessed for the church at Corinth.[8] They were likeminded. In that sense Titus was much like Timothy (cf. Phil. 2:20). Both had a genuine concern for others.

8. The Greek word for "earnest care" is the same as that for "diligence" (8:7) and "forwardness" (8:8).

Paul had sent Titus originally from Ephesus, and the associate went "with fear and trembling" (7:15). Now he was anxious to return because God had created a special love within his heart for the Corinthians. He missed them. When the apostle exhorted him to go back to Corinth from Macedonia with the epistle of II Corinthians, he enthusiastically accepted the opportunity. Paul, however, wanted to make it absolutely clear that Titus was going "of his own accord."[9]

He asked Paul to charge him to go back. In fact, Paul admitted that Titus had a greater enthusiasm for the Corinthians than the apostle did himself ("being more forward").[10] Since Paul's heart was enlarged to encompass all of the church (6:11), that was a striking testimonial to the size of Titus' heart.

2. The brother (8:18–19)

Titus was accompanied by "the brother," who also was sent by Paul. Who is this nameless person? No one can be dogmatic, but most speculation centers around Luke.[11] On the second missionary journey, Luke joined Paul at Troas and traveled to Philippi, where he remained when the apostle moved on to Thessalonica (Acts 16:10–17:1). Now, on his first trip back into Macedonia, it is plausible that Paul was rejoined by Luke.[12]

9. The phrase "of his own accord" comes from the same Greek word as "willing" (8:3).

10. This phrase is a comparative form of the word mentioned in footnote 8: *spoudaioteros.*

11. Robertson implies that Luke "may also be the brother of Titus." A. T. Robertson, *Word Pictures in the New Testament,* 6 vols. (Nashville: Broadman Press, 1931), 4:245.

12. Luke, the author of Acts, included himself in the events by the usage of the first person plural personal pronouns: "we" and "us." Note the resumption in Acts 20:5–6.

This anonymous brother is commended in two areas. *First,* all of the churches gave him "praise." He was well known and esteemed highly wherever he labored "in the gospel." There were no negative criticisms about his life and ministry. *Second,* he was "chosen" by the churches to travel with Paul, to assist the apostle in gathering the collection, and to carry the gift to Jerusalem. The word "chosen" literally means "to stretch out the hand" *(cheirotonētheis).* By a public vote through the raising of hands, he was selected and appointed by the churches to this task. This corporate choice shows that churches in the first century cooperated to achieve common goals. They did not always act independently of each other.

The importance of the collection was again stressed. It is "this grace" (cf. 8:7). It was "administered" by Paul and his associates; it was not for them. It was designed to bring glory to God and to manifest the loving concern of willing hearts.

3. Our brother (8:22)

Another anonymous messenger is mentioned. He was not Paul's physical brother, but rather a brother in Christ. Perhaps it was Silas or Apollos, but no one knows for sure. Two outstanding qualities about him are enumerated. *First,* he was "proved diligent in many things." He had been tested as to his zeal, ability, and faithfulness on many occasions, and in each situation Paul saw that he had excelled. His performance in Christian service qualified him for this important task. *Second,* he had an ardent zeal to see the collection finalized and taken to Jerusalem. Thus, Paul believed that this brother could help the other two to guide the Corinthians in the fulfillment of their pledge ("now much more diligent, upon the great confidence which I have in you").

B. Their Responsibility (8:20–21)

Although Paul trusted himself and knew that God trusted him, he wanted to remain above reproach. In the first epistle (chapter 9), he informed the Corinthians that he was not in the ministry for what he could get out of it. He never took their money, nor did he handle any.

Now that a large sum of money was being collected, he assured everyone that he would not use it for his own selfish gratification once he was away from that region. He wanted to "avoid blame." Although he had the general oversight ("which is administered by us"), he appointed others to gather and hold the money. He knew that it would be a sizeable amount ("abundance"). He also wanted the church to know that the messengers were not all "hand picked" by him. The churches bore the responsibility for the selection of some of the messengers (8:19, 23). Paul knew that he was under constant scrutiny by his critics; therefore, he did not want to give them any grounds for the slightest suspicion of wrongdoing.

Thus, he was "providing for honest things." The word for "honest" *(kala)* refers to what has a good outward appearance. He knew that God looked on his heart ("not only in the sight of the Lord"), but that was not sufficient. Since men look on the outward appearance, so the apostle wanted the welfare collection to appear right "in the sight of men."

C. Their Accreditation (8:23)

Because some opponents still remained in the church, he felt constrained to commend these messengers. Since the church was impressed with letters of commendation (3:1), he now gave them one.

He identified Titus as his "partner" *(koinōnos).* They shared a common love for the spiritual welfare of the church. He was also a "fellowhelper concerning you." Both Paul and Titus had worked in the city of Corinth. They complemented each other's ministry.

The two anonymous brothers are called "the messengers of the churches." The word "messengers" is *apostoloi,* normally translated as "apostles." It was used in the nontechnical sense in that they had been commissioned directly by the churches to be treasurers of the collection. They had not seen the resurrected Christ and had not been appointed to the apostolic gospel ministry (cf. I Cor. 9:1). But they both lived and served for "the glory of Christ," not for the furtherance of themselves or of the reputation of Paul.

D. Their Reception (8:24)

In this verse, he admonished the church to receive the messengers. *First,* they were to be a testimony both to the messengers and to their sending churches. They were to be kind and hospitable. *Second,* they were to show "the proof" of their love for the poor and for Paul by the completion of their financial commitment. *Third,* they were to vindicate Paul's boasting over their good spiritual qualities and over their initial zeal to give (7:14). He wanted the Corinthians to manifest in deed what he had said about them.

QUESTIONS FOR DISCUSSION

1. Do Christians give enough of their money to the Lord through their churches? Are they liberal? What can be done to improve the quality and quantity of giving?

2. Do many view giving as a grace gift? Should giving be forced upon people?

3. Is tithing taught in this passage? Should giving be restricted to a certain percentage of income?

4. Should Christians save money for retirement or to give to their heirs? How much should be saved for the future? Should they will some of their money to Christian causes?

5. How can equality of giving be maintained? What should our obligation be to poor believers in needy places?

6. Should pastors handle the money in local churches? Should the treasurer(s) of a church be selected on financial ability alone?

7. How can Christians, ministers, and churches improve their image about money before the world? Should collections be taken at evangelistic meetings? What about public audits?

9

The Characteristics of Biblical Giving

II Corinthians 9

The subject of giving covers two entire chapters within this epistle, the most concentrated section on the topic found anywhere in the Scriptures. In an explanation and defense of the collection, Paul continued to set forth concepts that should be incorporated within the giving program of all believers and of all churches.

David made this observation: "Blessed is he that considereth the poor: the Lord will deliver him in time of trouble" (Ps. 41:1). To give to those who cannot reciprocate is to give as God gives. When a believer learns to give in this way, then he will know what giving is all about. In this chapter, the apostle dealt with three major characteristics of such giving.

I. THE TESTIMONY OF GIVING (9:1–5)

This paragraph of verses actually continues the discussion concerning the sending of the three messengers (8:16–24). Paul had just admonished them to show the proof of their love (8:24). Now, he elaborated upon that demonstration. Their testimony was in the spotlight. Would it be positive or negative? Paul wanted it to be the former.

A. To Others (9:1–2)

1. Awareness of responsibility (9:1)

One reason why many believers have a poor testimony before others is their ignorance of their responsibilities. They simply do not know what they should do or how they should feel in certain situations. They need to be taught biblical directives and be shown a personal example to follow. In their immaturity, they need to grow in grace through experience.

This, however, was not the problem at Corinth. They *were aware* of their responsibilities, and they knew what had to be done. Up to this point, they simply had not done it.

Paul admitted: ". . . it is superfluous for me to write to you." It was not necessary for them to be reminded of their financial obligations; nevertheless, he did it anyway. In the past, procedural instructions had been included in the first epistle (I Cor. 16:1–4). Titus had already encouraged them once (8:6). Now, they would have the guidance of the three messengers plus the teaching of these two chapters (8-9).

He informed them that their collection involved "the ministering to the saints."[1] Christ ministered by giving His life on the cross (Matt. 20:28). Paul and Apollos ministered through evangelism and teaching (I Cor. 3:5). Now they could minister by giving their money. Specifically, it was a ministry "to the saints." They themselves were saints (1:1; cf. I Cor. 1:2); thus they should have compasssion upon those of their own kind (Gal. 6:10). Elsewhere, Paul wrote: "Bear ye one another's burdens, and so fulfil the

1. The words "as touching" come from the familiar preposition *peri*, which Paul used to introduce the various topics included in their letter to him (I Cor. 7:1, 25; 8:1; 12:1; 16:1, 12).

law of Christ" (Gal. 6:2). Family members should care for each other's financial needs. It is written: "But if any provide not for his own, and specially for those of his own house, he hath denied the faith, and is worse than an infidel" (I Tim. 5:8; cf. James 1:27).

2. Influence upon others (9:2)

The church, however, may not have known that Paul used it as an illustrative pattern to stimulate other churches to give to the welfare collection. Now, he wanted them to know that other churches had looked to the Corinthians for financial leadership in this project. They had a real influence upon others even though they might have been unaware of it.

The church at Corinth originally was very enthusiastic about the project. They wanted to give, and they desired that the amount be considerable. Paul was aware of this initial zeal ("For I know the forwardness of your mind").

He had, in fact, boasted about their willful commitment to the Macedonian churches. He was still glorying in them and in what they promised to do at the writing of this very epistle ("for which I boast of you to them of Macedonia").[2] He had not given up on them. He knew that they would do what they had covenanted to give.

He informed the other churches "that Achaia was ready a year ago." This does not mean that the money had already been collected; rather, it points out that the church had finalized their plans for giving. They had set a goal for themselves and they knew how much money would have to be set aside weekly to reach the goal before Paul arrived. Although the church at Corinth established the treasury for this collection, other Christians in the region

2. Note the present tense "I boast" *(kauchomai).*

of Achaia volunteered their assistance (1:1). The Roman province of Achaia included the Isthmus of Corinth and all land to the south of it.

Paul then told them: ". . . your zeal hath provoked [stimulated] very many." The original enthusiastic commitment of the Corinthians thus stirred and excited the churches of Macedonia and Galatia to join them. At the beginning of the collection, then, the church at Corinth had been the pioneers and had widely blessed and challenged others by their testimony.

B. To Themselves (9:3–5)

Paul did not want the church to lose this good testimony before the other churches. He and his associates knew that their collection so far had been a failure. Yet in spite of all the friction between Paul and the church, he had never revealed this information to the other churches. He did not want to embarrass the Corinthian church, nor did he want to jeopardize the collection.

1. To vindicate his boasting (9:3)

Out of his love for them and concern for their outward testimony, he "sent the brethren." The main mission of these three was to finalize the Corinthian collection.

He did not want his boasting about them to be "in vain," or his words to be empty, void of substantiation. He hoped that his confession would be supported by their practice.

He wanted them to "be ready" in performance as they had been ready in plans.[3] The apostle had gone out on the

3. The verb "may be ready" is *pareskeusmenoi hēte,* the usage of the perfect passive participle with the present subjunctive of *eimi* ("to be").

proverbial limb for them ("as I said"). They could either vindicate his confidence in them or bring suspicion upon the integrity of his words. If the Corinthians had failed, then the other churches could have thought that the apostle manipulated them with a challenging example that was not true.

2. To avoid shame (9:4)

He did not wish them or himself to be shamed before the Macedonians. He speculated that some of the Macedonians might accompany him to Corinth ("lest haply if they of Macedonia come with me"). Since the churches of northern Greece had been stimulated by the Corinthians, it would be very likely that they would send representatives to see and to thank the church at Corinth for their good example. When Paul traveled to Jerusalem with the money, he was accompanied by Sopater of Berea and by Aristarchus and Secundus of Thessalonica (Acts 20:4). Thus, it is very plausible that these appointed trustees of the collection did go to Corinth with Paul.

He did not want these Macedonian brothers to find them "unprepared." If they did, he knew that he personally would be embarrassed ("we should be ashamed"). In a parenthetical thought, he inserted that they would also be ashamed, but not as much as himself ("that we say not, ye"). It would be similar to a situation where a father bragged about the basketball exploits of his son to a college recruiter. When the son then missed five shots in a row, who would be more embarrassed, the father or the son?

It was Paul who had boasted about them; they had not boasted about themselves ("in this same confident boasting"). The word "confident" *(hupostasei)* refers to a foundation or substratum. For example, faith is the "substance [same word] of things hoped for, the evidence of things not seen" (Heb. 11:1). The apostle believed that the Corinthians would give sufficiently to fulfill their pledge; therefore, he built his boasting upon that foundation of faith. He trusted that he would see the money they promised to give. He staked his reputation on it.

3. To keep the blessing (9:5)

To maintain their testimony and to avoid embarrassment, the church needed to complete the collection. They also needed the blessing of voluntary giving. This is why Paul "thought it necessary" to send the three messengers (cf. 9:3). Much was at stake concerning their life and witness. It is better not to make a vow than to make one and fail to keep it (Eccles. 5:4–5).

The advance team then was sent for two purposes.[4] *First,* they were to prepare the way for the apostle's visit ("they would go before unto you"). *Second,* they were to "make up beforehand your bounty." The verb "make up" *(prokatartisōsi)* is used for the mending of fishers' nets and for the setting of broken bones. Their collection procedure was disconnected. The messengers were sent to assist them in putting the contribution back together.

Paul wanted their collection to be "a matter of bounty, and not as of covetousness." The word "bounty" is normally translated as "blessing" *(eulogia).* The church had been blessed when it made its original, voluntary commitment. They wanted to give just to give (cf. 8:10–12). Now, Paul desired that they finish the project for the same reason. He was afraid that they might give just to get ("of covetousness"). He did not want them to give because they

4. Shown by the purpose connective *hina* ("that") with two subjunctive verbs.

felt forced to do so by his intense desire for the completion of the project.

II. THE PRINCIPLES OF GIVING (9:6–9)

To distinguish between giving as a matter of blessing ("bounty") and that of "covetousness," the apostle further elaborated upon the principles that permeate genuine biblical giving ("But this I say," cf. 8:1–15). Jesus commented on the difference with these words:

> Therefore when thou doest thine alms, do not sound a trumpet before thee, as the hypocrites do in the synagogues and in the streets, that they may have glory of men. Verily I say unto you, They have their reward.
>
> But when thou doest alms, let not thy left hand know what thy right hand doeth:
>
> That thine alms may be in secret: and thy Father which seeth in secret himself shall reward thee openly (Matt. 6:2–4).

To give to impress men is to give out of covetousness; to give from thanking God is to give out of blessing.

A. Within Proper Attitudes (9:6–7)

1. It should be done bountifully (9:6)

There is a biblical principle that is true in all life's situations: ". . . whatsoever a man soweth, that shall he also reap" (Gal. 6:7). This applies to sinful living, to godly living, and to giving (Gal. 6:8). A person reaps *in kind* what he has sown and he reaps *more* than what he has sown. He only reaps what he sown, not that which he has stored. The more he sows, the more he reaps.

Thus, little giving will reap little blessing, and much giving will reap much blessing. The contrast is between "sparingly" and "bountifully" (literally, "on the basis of blessings," *ep eulogiais)*.

This principle corroborates the teaching of Christ: "Give, and it shall be given unto you; good measure, pressed down, and shaken together, and running over, shall men give unto your bosom. For with the same measure that ye mete withal it shall be measured to you again" (Luke 6:38). Solomon confirmed it: "The liberal soul shall be made fat, and he that watereth shall be watered also himself" (Prov. 11:25).

2. It should be done purposefully (9:7a)

Christians should not give with impromptu thoughtlessness. Rather, it should be done according to the standard of voluntary, planned determination ("according as he purposeth"). The word "purposeth" means "to choose beforehand" *(proaireitai).* All the giving by a believer should point back to a time when he made a decision before God to give himself and his substance to the Lord.[5]

The purposefulness must originate within the "heart." It must be self-originated, not in a forced conformity to a plan devised by others.

No believer is exempt from giving. The minister and the church member, the missionary and the national believer, and the poor and the rich all can give in this fashion ("every man").

3. It should be done joyfully (9:7b)

Three characteristics are mentioned: two negative and one positive. *First,* money should not be given "grudgingly." Literally, it means "out of grief, sorrow, or pain" *(ek lupēs).* This type of giver hurts when giving. He knows that he must, but he winces when the collection plate is

5. The verb is in the perfect tense, which stresses a past completed action with results of that action continuing into the present.

passed. He grieves the loss of his money. He is reluctant to part with it. To him, the giving of little is really the giving of too much.

Second, giving should not be "of necessity." Although Paul informed them about their obligation to give, he did not want them to give out of necessity (9:5). A person gives in this way when he wonders what others expect him to give or what others will think about him if he does not give. If he feels pressured to give, then he gives out of necessity. To keep up appearances, Ananias and Sapphira gave publicly, but they did not give what they promised to give. They kept back what they pledged to God and suffered fatally for it (Acts 5:1–11).

Third, a believer should be a "cheerful giver." The word "cheerful" comes from a Greek word *(hilaron),* which is literally "hilarious." It is also related to the word used for "propitiation" (cf. I John 2:2). Just as God was satisfied with the payment of Christ's voluntary death on the cross, so He loves the believer who satisfies Him with gifts of love and thanksgiving.

B. With Proper Acknowledgment (9:8–9)

1. To divine sufficiency (9:8)

Many Christians do not give enough or in the right attitude because they are afraid that there will not be enough money left to pay the bills. Regardless of the admonitions of Scripture and the testimonies of dedicated Christians, they still are not convinced that they can do it. They lack faith in the ability of God to meet their financial needs.

Such givers must take a good look at God's omnipotence. Only God can give believers confidence ("And God is able to make all grace abound toward you"). They must be overwhelmed by what God through divine grace has given to them before they will be in a position to give properly. God can change the "Ebenezer Scrooge" attitude within believers by the influence of the indwelling Holy Spirit through the Scriptures.

Believers must understand that God can supply the needs of the giver after the gift has been given ("that ye always having all sufficiency in all things"). Only those who have given sacrificially and voluntarily, like the Macedonians, can claim the promise of this verse: "But my God shall supply all your need according to his riches in glory by Christ Jesus" (Phil. 4:19; cf. 4:14–18). There are no exceptions to this all-inclusive provision of God.[6]

The word "sufficiency" literally means "self rule" *(autarkeian).* Regardless of his financial condition, Paul learned to be "content" (same word; Phil. 4:11). He learned to have his needs met when he had little money and when he had much money. He knew that he could do it "through Christ which strengtheneth [him]" (Phil. 4:13). Many Christians are ruled by a desire to be secure financially (I Tim. 6:6–9). For this reason, they do not put godliness first in their lives (cf. Matt. 6:25–34). For this reason, they have anxiety about money and giving.

God can cause the believer to "abound to every good work" if he gives properly. A giving Christian will find that God will prosper him in all areas of living. The joy of giving will permeate his entire lifestyle.

2. *To divine faithfulness (9:9)*

The sovereignty of God and the will of men work harmoniously together in the provision of men's needs. God meets these needs through the free, loving concern of other men. It is God who "hath given to the poor" (cf. Ps.

6. Note the threefold usage of "all" plus the singular usage of "every" in this verse.

112:9). God must receive glory and thanksgiving, but men also share in that praise.

God is righteous in that He faithfully fulfills His promise to supply man's needs. This is a holy, eternal pledge (9:9b). David said: "I have been young, and now am old; yet have I not seen the righteous forsaken, nor his seed begging bread" (Ps. 37:25).

The believer must recognize that while he is on earth he is a steward of God's money and provision. Someone has said: "It is not how much of my money I give to the Lord, but rather, how much of His money I keep for myself." The Christian must see that he might be the very instrument that God wants to use to supply the needs of another.

III. THE BLESSINGS OF GIVING (9:10–15)

Jesus Christ said: "It is more blessed to give than to receive" (Acts 20:35). Most would rather receive than give simply because they have never matured into this spiritual experience. In their narrow world of self-expression, they cannot perceive that giving is better than getting.

A. For Self (9:10)

The saint who gives will come to know intimately the God who provides. God is "he that ministereth seed to the sower" (Isa. 55:10). God controls the cycle of nature for man's provision. He created plant and animal life, water, air, and the seed-plant-fruit cycle. He is also the source of the money that man receives and gives.

Three statements are made about His provision. *First,* He "ministers bread for food."

Second, He "multiplies your seed sown." Christ said: "Except a corn of wheat fall into the ground and die, it abideth alone: but if it die, it bringeth forth much fruit"

(John 12:24). There are no dividends from seed in the storage bins. It must be invested (planted) into the earth to produce a harvest. Solomon wrote: "He that hath pity upon the poor lendeth unto the Lord; and that which he hath given will he pay him again" (Prov. 19:17). The money that Christians give is like seed sown. It will come back in a multiplied harvest of spiritual blessings.

Third, He will "increase the fruits of your righteousness." A miserly believer cannot grow much spiritually. A mature child of God will also be a liberal giver. He will not feel compelled to give. He will respond willingly whenever needs are prayerfully presented to him. The more he gives, the more righteous he will become.

B. For Others (9:11–14)

Everyone is blessed by giving: the giver, the recipient, and those who observe. The giver will not only be directly blessed in his act of giving, but he will receive future blessing through the giving of thanks by others for him. It is a moving experience to have someone say: "Thank you for all that you have done."

1. By Paul (9:11)

Through the practice of biblical principles of giving, the Corinthians would constantly be "enriched in everything to all bountifulness."[7] Instead of becoming impoverished through giving, as they might have expected, they would actually become spiritual plutocrats *(ploutizomenoi).* The word "bountifulness" *(haplotēta)* refers to their liberality, comparable to that of the Macedonians (8:2). They would be rich in giving, wealthy in liberality. Those are genuine riches.

7. The participle "being enriched" is in the present tense. Since it is in the nominative case, it must grammatically refer to "ye" (9:8).

When that took place, Paul assured them that he would thank God for them and for their contribution to the welfare collection ("which causeth through us thanksgiving to God"). In addition, he would thank God for what He had done in their lives.

2. By the Jerusalem church (9:12–14)

Through the completion of their project, Paul anticipated four blessings that would fall upon them and upon the Jerusalem church. *First,* the poor Christian Jews in Palestine would have their needs met ("supplieth the want of the saints," 9:12a). The word "supplieth" *(esti prosanaplērousa)* means to fill up by adding to. It was up to the Corinthians to add to the total already given so that the goal would be completely reached. Although they were the first to pledge, they would actually be the last to give. The word "service" comes from the Greek *leitourgias,* which transliterates as "liturgy." It refers to a public religious service either in priestly ministry (Luke 1:23) or in humble service to others (Phil. 2:30).

Second, the poor saints would give thanks to God for His gracious provision ("but is abundant also by many thanksgivings unto God" (9:12b). When one person keeps his money, then one person can give thanks; when some of the money is given to others, then "many" persons can give thanks.

Third, the church at Jerusalem would glorify God and be thankful for the church at Corinth (9:13). They would give thanks for the obedience of the Corinthians ("professed subjection unto the gospel of Christ"). They would also give thanks for the liberal gift delivered "unto them, and unto all men." As they would thank God, the church at Corinth would be blessed by God.

Fourth, the poor saints would pray for the Corinthians (9:14). The Greek church would have gained the prayer support of believers in distant Jerusalem. Through this intercessory effort, they would become spiritually stronger.

C. For God (9:15)

When a believer gives to others, he begins to appreciate what God has given to him. This "thanks" goes beyond health, family, and money. As he gives, he will always thank God "for his unspeakable gift" (cf. John 3:16). Nothing can compare with the gift of eternal life through Jesus Christ. John wrote: "Beloved, if God so loved us, we ought also to love one another" (I John 4:11). The adverb "so" involves the essence of giving.

Did the Corinthians obey? Yes, they finalized their contribution and doubtless received the blessings that Paul listed (cf. Rom. 15:26–27). No one from Corinth, however, traveled with Paul to Jerusalem to deliver the money personally.[8]

8. In Acts 20:4, no one from Corinth is mentioned in the travel team.

QUESTIONS FOR DISCUSSION

1. Are some Christians shamed into giving? If so, what methods are used to produce such embarrassment?

2. Should churches cooperate more in group money-raising projects? For what causes should they unite? Who should be in charge of the money?

3. If the government would take away the tax deductible status of church contributions, would the amount of giving decrease or increase? Why?

4. Do these chapters support the principle of tithing? Can a believer purpose in his heart to give a tithe?

5. Why do people give grudgingly or out of necessity? How can these pressures be eliminated?

6. Why are Christians afraid to give more? Do they equate luxuries with needs?

7. Should records be kept of individual giving? Does this violate the concept of secrecy (Matt. 6:3)?

10

The Defense of Paul's Apostleship

II Corinthians 10

Throughout the entire epistle Paul presented an emotional apology for the integrity of his life and ministry. He has already defended his absence and conduct (1:1–2:13), his ministry (2:14–7:16), and his administration of the collection (8:1–9:15). Now he must prove the authenticity of his apostleship (chapters 10-13). The opposition of the minority, led and influenced by the Judaizers, forced him to do so. This was not a new experience, because throughout his epistles he demonstrated that he was a genuine apostle (I Cor. 4:9–21; 15:8–11; Gal. 1:1–2:14; Phil. 3:1–9; I Thess. 2:1–20; I Tim. 1:1–20).

I. HIS ACTIVITIES (10:1–6)

The opening words ("Now I Paul myself") show that Paul, not his associates, was under attack.[1] Whenever he wanted to make a strong assertion, he usually used such words (cf. Gal. 5:2). The ministry of the associates, of course, could be undermined if their apostolic leader could

1. Robertson speculated: "It may be that at this point he took the pen from the amanuensis and wrote himself as in Gal. 6:11." A. T. Robertson, *Word Pictures in the New Testament,* 6 vols. (Nashville: Broadman Press, 1931), 4:251.

be discredited. In a sense, therefore, Paul's defense of himself is a broader defense of his entire team.

Unfortunately, outward behavior is easily misinterpreted. For example, shyness is often identified as genuine humility, or an inquisitive questioner is viewed as a critical person. Paul thus had to show that his activities truly represented genuine apostleship.

A. He Expressed the Qualities of Christ (10:1–2a)

Christ delegated His authority to the apostles. He sent them out to do what He had done (Matt. 10:1–8; 28:18–20; John 20:21–23; Acts 1:8). He also sent them out to perform their ministries with the same inner spiritual qualities that He had.

1. Humility (10:1a)

Christ was concerned about the needs of people, and so was Paul. That is why he implored them to be responsive to him ("I Paul myself beseech you"). Just as Christ wept over Jerusalem and invited burdened sinners to come to Him, so Paul shed tears over the rebellious Corinthians and urged them to be reconciled to him.

In His life and service, Christ was marked by "meekness and gentleness." These two qualities reflect two directions of the same virtue of humility.[2] The attribute of "meekness" *(praotētos)* is the humility of self before God, whereas the characteristic of "gentleness" *(epieikeias)* is humility in the treatment of others. Christ claimed to be "meek and lowly in heart" (Matt. 11:29). He declared: "Blessed are the meek" (Matt. 5:5). He was pliable under the will of God. He was tender and approachable before men. It was

2. The Granville Sharp rule of grammar applies here. Only one article appears with the two nouns joined by "and" *(kai)*.

predicted of Him: "A bruised reed shall he not break, and smoking flax shall he not quench" (Matt. 12:20). But meekness must not be confused with weakness. Christ was not afraid to stand up for His convictions. Meekness, in fact, is power under control. The ox is meek when it is in the yoke. Thus, a believer has a real power and true meekness when he is under the yoke of the will of God.

The attribute of "gentleness" is marked by reasonableness. A pastor should not be a "striker" (I Tim. 3:3). Believers should not be "brawlers, but gentle, showing all meekness unto all men" (Titus 3:2). If a man possesses the wisdom of God, he will be gentle (James 3:17). A gentle believer will not seek revenge out of personal meanness. Christ prayed for and forgave His mockers (Luke 23:34).

Concerning himself, Paul then said: ". . . who in presence am base among you." The word "base" *(tapeinos)* can have both a bad and a good sense. Christ used it of Himself when He said that He was "lowly in heart" (Matt. 11:29). The verbal form of the word is used in this exhortation: "Humble yourselves in the sight of the Lord" (James 4:10). The critics, however, misinterpreted and misrepresented Paul's humble demeanor. In a derogatory sense, they accused Paul of being faint hearted, which is not a characteristic of true apostleship.

2. Boldness (10:1b–2)

His opponents charged Paul with being inconsistent. They said that he was "base" when he was in Corinth and "bold" only when he was away from the city. According to their supposition, from a safe distance only did Paul try to scare the church with stern letters (10:9–10).

The apostle, of course, denied this criticism. There is no contradiction between humility and an authoritative boldness. Christ had both. He embraced children and also drove out the money changers from the temple. Circumstances dictated which characteristic should be publicly manifested.

The same was true of Paul. When he was in Corinth the first two times, he used the humble approach. When he wrote the tearful letter, he was forced to demonstrate his apostolic authority. He now claimed that he would manifest his apostolic boldness at his next visit upon those who resisted him ("wherewith I think to be bold against some"). These critics charged that Paul's differences in behavior proved that he "walked according to the flesh" and not according to the Holy Spirit.

To avoid using his apostolic discipline, he begged them to submit to his authority in advance ("But I beseech you"). He stated that he did not plan to use his authority upon those who did not need it ("that I may not be bold when I am present with you").

B. He Employed the Methods of Christ (10:2–6)

The critics charged that Paul "walked according to the flesh," that his techniques for solving church and personal problems were selfishly motivated.

1. They were not worldly (10:3)

Paul explained the difference between walking "according to the flesh" *(kata sarka)* and walking "in the flesh" *(en sarki).* The latter merely indicates mortal existence. For example, Christ became flesh and walked as a man in the midst of men.

Paul denied that he warred according to the flesh.[3] The word "war" is a military term, which he used to introduce

3. The two prepositions "according to" and "after" come from the same Greek word *kata.*

the concept of spiritual conflict. The term "war" *(strateuometha),* transliterated as "strategy," was used of the tactics of the general who led his army into battle. But Paul did not purpose (1:17), walk (Rom. 8:4), or live according to the flesh (Rom. 8:13). His walk was controlled by the Holy Spirit, not by the fleshly sin nature (Rom. 8:4; Gal. 5:16).

2. They were divinely effective (10:4–5)

He then claimed that "the weapons of our warfare were not carnal." The word "warfare" refers to plans of strategy whereas the word "weapons" *(hopla)* points to the military hardware needed to carry out the plans. In that day, they would have included bows and arrows, catapults, and swords. Today, the weapons would be guns, tanks, submarines, airplanes, and ballistic missiles. A Christian should not walk according to human plans, nor should he attempt to carry out divine plans with worldly means.

His weapons, rather, were "mighty" *(dunata).* They came from God and were designed to bring glory to God ("through God"). This intrinsic power came from the indwelling Holy Spirit who controlled the apostle's life (Acts 1:8). These divine weapons achieved permanent results ("to the pulling down of strong holds"). The word "pulling down" *(kathairesin)* was used militarily of the destruction of fortress walls by ramming, rock throwing, and undermining.

Paul overcame opposition both at Corinth and elsewhere through the spiritual means of intercessory prayer, tearful admonition by his presence and pen, and the compassionate appeals of his associates. David overcame Goliath with the sling and stone, not with Saul's armor and sword. Gideon won with only pitchers, torches, and trumpets. The walls of Jericho fell as Israel walked around the city in obedient faith. Genuine believers know the truth of this spiritual axiom: "Not by might, nor by power, but by my spirit, saith the Lord of hosts" (Zech. 4:6).

Paul then internalized the spiritual conflict. The real battle for a believer takes place within his soul. In his struggle to be holy, will he have victory or defeat? A victorious saint will achieve two goals.[4] *First,* he will be successful in "casting down imaginations, and every high thing that exalteth itself against the knowledge of God" (10:5a). After a sinner has been saved and the believing sinner has yielded himself to God (Rom. 12:1), he must maintain constant vigilance over his thought life. After ancient cities were conquered, often there were insurrections and attempts to rebuild the destroyed walls. A believer must continually suppress unregenerate, proud

4. This is indicated by the usage of two participles "casting" and "bringing."

The southeast corner of the old city wall at Jerusalem.

thoughts and plans that would rebel against holy, spiritual knowledge.

Second, he must bring "into captivity every thought to the obedience of Christ" (10:5b). He must saturate his mind and will with biblical truth. He must think as Christ would think. He must act as Christ would act. Only then can he say with Paul: "For to me to live is Christ" (Phil. 1:21). He must think on that which is true, honest, just, pure, lovely, good, virtuous, and praiseworthy (Phil. 4:8).

3. They were flexible (10:6)

In conquered cities, the inhabitants were treated according to their subordination to the victors. The Romans permitted many cities to govern their own affairs (e.g. Ephesus), whereas procurators and armies were assigned to keep the peace in troublesome places (e.g. Jerusalem).

Paul viewed the evangelization of Corinth and the subsequent revival as spiritual conquests. He planned to honor the obedience of the majority with a humble, paternal ministry ("when your obedience is fulfilled"). The obedience of the complete church could not be finalized, however, until the rebellious minority had been suppressed. He informed the church and the insurrectionists that he possessed "a readiness to revenge all disobedience." Upon his arrival, he planned to deal severely with the dissidents. The only way that they could escape such firm apostolic discipline was to repent before he came.

II. HIS AUTHORITY (10:7–11)

Things often are not what they appear to be. The church stressed "outward appearance." Literally, it means "the things that are according to face" *(ta kata prosōpon).* It refers to what can be seen or heard. The critics charged that Paul did not have the appearance of an apostle.[5] According to them, he did such nonapostolic things as working with his hands and weeping before others.

A. His Authority Came From Christ (10:7)

The Bible rejects outward evaluation as the final standard for estimating worth. The prophet Samuel was rebuked by God for thinking that Eliab would be the next king of Israel after Saul: "Look not on his countenance, or on the height of his stature; because I have refused him: for the Lord seeth not as man seeth; for man looketh on the outward appearance, but the Lord looketh on the heart" (I Sam 16:7).

Paul affirmed that he belonged to Christ and that he was sent from Christ ("even so are we Christ's). Elsewhere, he stated that he was "an apostle, not of men, neither by man, but by Jesus Christ" (Gal. 1:1). He was the least deserving to be an apostle, but nevertheless, he was a genuine apostle equal to the others (I Cor. 15:9–10).

The person who claimed to be of Christ but who questioned Paul's spiritual background needed to re-examine the facts ("if any man trust to himself that he is Christ's, let him of himself think this again"). This might refer to the believer who heard Christ during His earthly ministry (cf. I Cor. 1:12). This one might have reported that Paul did not speak or act like Christ did.

B. His Authority Was for Edification (10:8)

Paul did not flaunt his high spiritual office. He did not display his apostleship before others. He saw himself as a humble servant of God and of people.

5. The verb "look" *(blepete)* can be either indicative or imperative. If the former, it can be either a declarative or an interrogative sentence. If the latter, it would mean that Paul challenged them to look at the facts with close scrutiny.

On the other hand, the critics, notably the Judaizers, constantly bragged about their achievements. To offset this egotistical group, Paul knew that he would have to "boast somewhat more" of his authority. Although he ordinarily did not do this, he said that he would not be ashamed to do so if needed ("I should not be ashamed").

Paul was a builder, not a destroyer (I Cor. 3:10; Eph. 2:20). Christ gave him such important authority "for edification." He built churches in areas where the redemptive work of Christ had never been preached before (Rom. 15:20). Although he possessed apostolic authority to discipline sinning members (I Cor. 5:3–5), he preferred to use it only as a last resort. He did not want to abuse his power. His purpose in writing, in preaching, and in the sending of his associates was not for their "destruction."[6] He wanted to build them up, not to tear them down (13:10). Construction involves time, planning, and patience, whereas destruction is usually quick and noisy.

C. His Authority Was Consistent (10:9–11)

Paul admitted to the possession of both humility in their presence and boldness in their absence (10:1). The critics took this obvious difference and misrepresented the apostle before the dissident minority.

1. The false charge (10:9–10)

They charged that Paul wanted to "terrify" the church by his epistles (10:9). They claimed that he tried to scare them into repentance. The usage of the plural "letters" shows that the apostle must have written two or three epistles before the composition of II Corinthians: the let-

6. This is the same Greek word, used for "pulling down" (10:4) and "casting down."

ter concerning fornication (I Cor. 5:9); I Corinthians; and the tearful, painful letter (2:3–4; 7:8). The critics ("say they") admitted that his letters were "weighty and powerful" (10:10). They recognized that what he wrote (content) and how he wrote (literary style) manifested the penmanship of one who claimed to be authoritative. They did not deny this. They, however, resisted that authority. They did what Peter declared:

> And account that the longsuffering of our Lord is salvation; even as our beloved brother Paul also according to the wisdom given unto him hath written unto you;
>
> As also in all his epistles, speaking in them of these things hard to be understood, which they that are unlearned and unstable wrest, as they do also the other scriptures, unto their own destruction (II Peter 3:16–17).

They charged, however, that Paul was ineffective when he stood before the church. In their estimation, his "bodily presence [was] weak, and his speech contemptible" (10:10b). To them Paul did not look like an apostle. He did have a defect (Gal. 4:14), a fleshly ailment unknown to us (12:7) and scars over his body caused by severe persecutions (11:24–25). Robertson reported: "In the second century *Acts of Paul and Theda* Paul is pictured as small, short, bow-legged, with eye-brows knit together and an aquiline nose."[7] The "weakness" could also refer to his humble demeanor. To the Greek way of thinking, both were repulsive.

They also claimed that he did not speak like an apostle. They elevated rhetorical eloquence, such as Apollos possessed (Acts 18:24). The word "contemptible" *(exouthenēmenos)* connoted what was treated as nothing (cf. I Cor. 1:28). Paul admitted that he was not a trained orator, but that did not diminish the spiritual wisdom and the authority of his words (11:6). They charged that he

7. Robertson, *Word Pictures,* 4:254.

did not communicate authoritative leadership when he spoke as when he wrote.

2. The charge refuted (10:11)

Paul then warned the leader ("such an one") of the critics ("say they," 10:10) that he would deal with the rebel severely when he arrived. Later, he threatened to discipline all who had rejected his apostolic authority (13:2, 10). He was not against using his rod of chastisement (I Cor. 4:21).

Paul promised that he would manifest the same authority that was revealed in his letters when he was personally present with them. If they wanted to see what real authority was like, he pledged that they would see it the next time they saw him. They would live to regret their critical attacks upon Paul.

III. HIS APPROVAL (10:12–18)

Paul earlier rejected the concept of commendation by self or by others (3:1–3). Now, he wished to show that he did not execute his apostolic office to suit the expectations of others, but rather to fulfill his commitment before God.

A. He Rejected Human Comparison (10:12)

1. The audacity of doing it (10:12a)

The opening words ("we dare not") show Paul's total rejection of this standard of approval. No spiritually minded person would dare make such an egotistical judgment (I Cor. 4:3–5). Who has the competence to do it?

The Judaizing critic, however, delighted in making such comparisons. *First,* he compared himself with his own self-appointed standard of excellence ("make ourselves of the number," *egkrinai).* This was introspection. *Second,* he compared himself with others ("with some that commend themselves," *sugkrinai).* This was competition. If a person adopts low standards for himself, he can usually meet them. If a person selects someone inferior with whom he can compare himself, he is bound to see himself as better.

2. The folly of doing it (10:12b)

The people who make such comparisons are "not wise." They make two fallacious determinations. *First,* they are "measuring themselves by themselves." As a group, they set up their own convictions and practices as criteria for excellence. Then, if other groups or individuals fail to meet those specifications, they reject them as failures. Since Paul did not conform to their code, the Judaizers rejected him. *Second,* they were "comparing themselves among themselves." Within their own framework, they then tried to see who the best Judaizing teacher was.

There are obvious breakdowns in such comparisons. As an illustration, who is the better athlete: the best pitcher in baseball or the best quarterback in football? Who is more important on the baseball team: the pitcher or the catcher? These ridiculous comparisons are too often carried into the realm of spiritual ministries.

B. He Welcomed Evaluation (10:13–16)

1. Of his responsibilities (10:13–14)

He refused to boast about what could not honestly be measured ("things without measure," *ametra).* It is misleading to compare a pastor with an evangelist or a missionary with a Bible professor.

He could boast ("glory," *kauchēsometha),* however, about his achievements within the will of God. God assigned to him specific responsibilities as an apostle to the Gentiles (Acts 9:15; Rom. 1:5; Gal. 2:7–9). He knew what he had to do. He had to measure himself by the standard that applied only to him. The will of God for him was "the measure of the rule which God hath distributed" to him. In a sense, Paul was like the sprinter who raced against the time clock and his best previous time rather than against other runners.

The will of God for Paul involved the evangelization of Corinth ("a measure to reach even unto you"). Apostolic authority over Corinth was assigned by God to him, not to any other apostle or to the false teachers.

He did not move into the territory assigned to others ("For we stretch not ourselves beyond our measure"). But the Judaizers had done this when they moved into Corinth and attempted to discredit Paul's ministry. Paul was the first to preach in Corinth ("for we are come as far as to you"). He was their only spiritual father (I Cor. 4:15). Others, who taught in the church, were building upon the foundation laid exclusively by him (I Cor. 3:10–11).

2. Of his future (10:15–16)

It was impossible to compare the pioneer evangelistic work of Paul with the results "of other men's labors" at Corinth. There was no way to compare Paul with Apollos or with Timothy or with Titus. It would be just as wrong to compare the productivity of the modern farmer with that of his grandfather who had to cut timber and remove stumps before he could work the land with his horse-drawn plow.

Paul did have "hope" that when the church achieved maturity ("when your faith is increased") they would recognize the tremendous achievements of his labor among them (10:15b). He wanted them to judge him according to the will of God for his life alone ("according to our rule abundantly").

It was the will of God ("his rule") for him to preach the gospel in places where the name of Christ had never been proclaimed (10:16a; cf. Rom. 15:20–24). It was not the will of God for him to take over another apostle's work ("not to boast in another man's line of things made ready to our hand"). But the false teachers had invaded his territory. Not once did they go into pagan provinces untouched by the gospel.

C. He Desired Divine Commendation (10:17–18)

This commendation comes by glorying in the Lord (10:17; cf. Jer. 9:23–24; I Cor. 1:31). No one should boast about his station in life or what he has done (I Cor. 1:26–28). Rather, he should boast about what God has done for him, in him, and through him.

Self-commendation is unacceptable before God (10:18a). Solomon wrote: "Let another man praise thee, and not thine own mouth; a stranger, and not thine own lips" (Prov. 27:2). People mostly brag by comparing themselves with other people. But if they would contrast themselves with God, they would see how far short of the divine standard they have come (Job 42:5–6; Isa. 6:5).

The "approved" Christian is one "whom the Lord commendeth." If God works in and through a life, He will commend that person. Paul desired and received the acceptance of God. He could truly say:

> I have therefore whereof I may glory through Jesus Christ in those things which pertain to God.
>
> For I will not dare to speak of any of those things which Christ hath not wrought by me, to make the Gentiles obedient, by word and deed (Rom. 15:17–18).

QUESTIONS FOR DISCUSSION

1. In what ways is religious authority wrongly expressed? How can church members deal with a pastor who has misused his power?

2. In what ways do believers walk after the flesh or war after the flesh? How can they be helped?

3. What are the major differences between shyness and meekness? Between leadership and dictatorship?

4. Why are Christians impressed with outward appearances? What appeals to them? How can this situation be improved?

5. In what ways do ministers and church members compare themselves today? Should there be contests within the church?

6. Should ministers be called "Reverend" or "Doctor"? Should honorary doctorates be conferred upon preachers? Are they done for right reasons?

7. How can a person know the specific will of God for his own life? How can he know whether he has made achievement within that will?

11

The Folly of Religious Bragging

II Corinthians 11:1-29

Paul resisted self-disclosure of his private life. He was reluctant to talk about his spiritual accomplishments lest someone think that he was bragging. He condemned it in others (3:1; 10:12).

Of necessity, however, he now found himself doing what he disliked. He asked for the indulgence of the church: "Would to God ye could bear with me a little in my folly" (11:1a). This wish, at the time of writing, turned into a reality at the time of reading ("and indeed bear with me," 11:1b).[1] If they had read this far into the epistle, he knew that his prayer had been answered.

I. HIS INTENSE JEALOUSY OVER THEM (11:2–12)

In itself, jealousy *(zēlos)* is not a sin. It can be either good or bad. God is jealous (Josh. 24:19). Believers should have a fervent, jealous zeal for God, such as Elijah had (I Kings 19:10, 14). A person should be jealous when he

1. There is a switch from the imperfect *(aneichesthe)* to the present *(anechesthe)* of the same verb. The second form can be either indicative or imperative. If the former, the prayer was answered; if the latter, he appealed to them to do what he had prayed for.

sees a loved one being turned away from obedient faith by false attractions.

A. His Warning (11:2–6)

Paul loved them as God loved them. He was jealous over them as God was (11:2a).

1. He wanted them to be pure (11:2)

All believers comprise the church, symbolically the bride of Christ, the future wife of the Lamb of God (Rev. 19:7–8; 21:10). As the spiritual father of the Corinthian saints, Paul had "espoused," or betrothed, his spiritual daughter to "one husband," namely Christ.[2] Although he had apostolic authority over the church, they were really engaged to be married to Christ, the Head of the church (Eph. 1:22–23).

He thus desired to present the church "as a chaste virgin to Christ." Although immorality, personal friction, and doctrinal problems existed in the church, positionally they were washed, sanctified, and justified (cf. I Cor. 6:11). Christ is presently cleansing the church "that he might present it to himself a glorious church, not having spot, or wrinkle, or any such thing; but that it should be holy and without blemish" (Eph. 5:26–27).

2. He cautioned them against Satan (11:3)

He expressed his "fear" over the wrong influence that the Judaizers had imposed on them. He equated their situation with the original temptation of Eve by Satan in the Garden of Eden (Gen. 3:1–7).[3] Satan "beguiled" or

2. The verb is in the middle voice, emphasizing Paul's personal interest in the betrothal.

3. This verse shows that Paul believed in the historical veracity of the Genesis account of the fall of man.

deceived her completely *(exēpatēsen)* through his subtle, devious methods. Just as Satan used the serpent, he was now using the Judaizers to corrupt their "minds" (literally, "thoughts," *noēmata;* cf. 10:5).

The phrase, "the simplicity that is in Christ," refers to the doctrine of salvation by grace through faith alone apart from circumcision and obedience to the Mosaic law. The Judaizers taught that faith in Christ alone could not save, but that circumcision was also necessary (Acts 15:1). When Eve began to reason with Satan, she at that moment failed to submit her thoughts to God (cf. 10:5). The concept of "simplicity" is achieved when one is totally obedient to Christ through the revealed Word of God.

3. He questioned their tolerance of error (11:4)

Paul wondered whether they would bear with him in his folly of religious bragging, and yet they had willingly put up with damnable teaching ("ye might well bear," cf. 11:1).

Three areas of error are isolated. *First,* someone was preaching "another Jesus."[4] The word "another" *(allon)* means another of the same kind (e.g., McIntosh and Red Delicious are apples [same kind] but are different varieties). The Judaizers emphasized the earthly ministry of Jesus, but did not stress the finality of redemption in His death and resurrection.

Second, the Corinthians were receiving "another spirit." This word "another" *(heteron)* means another of a different kind (e.g., Pears and apples are both fruit, but of different kinds). When Paul evangelized them, they received the Holy Spirit, who produced liberty (3:17), love

4. The usage of *ei* ("if") with the indicative verbs shows that it was presently taking place. The usage of the singular may refer to the leader of the Judaizers (cf. 10:11).

(Gal. 5:22), and power (II Tim. 1:7) within them. The Judaizers, however, manifested the spirit of the world (I Cor. 2:12), or the spirit of bondage (Gal. 2:4).

Third, the Judaizers preached "another gospel" *(heteron).* The addition of works, either prior to or after faith, is a false requirement for salvation. Whenever self-effort is added, the efficacy of faith is eliminated (Gal. 2:21). Such proponents of error are under the curse of God (Gal. 1:6–9).

4. He vindicated his apostleship (11:5–6)

Paul reasoned that his abilities were comparable to those of the "very chiefest apostles." Although this was true in relation to the original twelve apostles (I Cor. 15:9–11), this phrase is an ironical reference to the previously mentioned false apostles (11:4; cf. 11:13–15).[5] These Judaizers constantly deprecated his physical appearance and pulpit effectiveness (10:10).

He admitted that he was not formally trained in oral rhetoric ("rude in speech"). The word "rude" *(idiōtēs)* refers to one who lacks professional training. The same charge was leveled at the apostles by the Jewish religious leaders: "Now when they saw the boldness of Peter and John, and perceived that they were unlearned and ignorant men *[idiōtai],* they marvelled" (Acts 4:13). Paul was a preacher, not a lecturer or dramatist! The worst pulpiteer is one who says nothing but says it well.

5. This is the view held by most evangelical commentators: R.V.G. Tasker, *The Second Epistle of Paul to the Corinthians,* Tyndale New Testament Commentaries (Grand Rapid: Wm. B. Eerdmans Publishing Co., 1960), p. 73; Philip E. Hughes, *Paul's Second Epistle to the Corinthians,* New International Commentary on the New Testament (Grand Rapids: Wm. B. Eerdmans Publishing Co., 1962), p. 379. Morgan, however, holds that Paul referred to genuine apostles. G. Campbell Morgan, *The Corinthian Letters of Paul* (Westwood, N.J.: Fleming H. Revell Co., 1956), p. 262.

Paul nonetheless had formal training "in knowledge." He had the best teacher anyone could have–Jesus Christ. Christ directly taught him everything he knew about the gospel (Gal. 1:11–12). In biblical content and spiritual application, he knew more about God's will than anyone else. This wisdom was a special divine gift to him (I Cor. 2:10–13; II Peter 3:15–16). Thus, what he said was true, logical, and authoritative.

The church should have recognized his apostolic authority and knowledge through his ministry in their midst (11:6b). When the Jews marveled and questioned the source of Christ's teachings, He replied: "My doctrine is not mine, but his that sent me. If any man will do his will, he shall know of the doctrine, whether it be of God, or whether I speak of myself" (John 7:15–17). If the church likewise determined to do the will of God, they would know that Paul was of God and that the Judaizers were of Satan.

B. His Financial Policy (11:7–12)

In the first epistle, he discussed extensively the reasons why he refused to be supported financially by them (I Cor. 9:1–18). As an apostle, he had the right to be paid for his services, but he chose not to exercise that right. Since salvation was a free gift, so was his preaching. He did not want people to think that he was exploiting them for material gain.

1. He lamented their misunderstanding (11:7–8)

The Judaizers and the dissident minority viewed his refusal to take an honorarium as an "offence" (literally "sin," *hamartian).* In the first century, professional speakers charged fees for their services. The greater the reputation, the higher the fee. The false teachers used

Paul's free speaking as an attack against his ability and his estimation of himself.

Paul, however, worked with his hands as a tentmaker to support himself. He did this in their best interest ("that ye might be exalted"). Paul, like Jesus, preached "freely." Christ never took an offering for His own support. He cautioned His apostles against ministering for financial gain (Matt. 10:9–10). He commanded them: ". . . freely ye have received, freely give" (Matt. 10:8).

Although Paul did not enlist support from the Corinthians when he was in their city, he did accept contributions from other churches at that time (11:8). The word "wages" *(opsōnion)* refers to money received by soldiers for the purchase of food rations. Other churches did for him what they should have done. This verse may indicate that although Paul did not demand money from them (which was his right), he would have accepted voluntary, unsolicited offerings from them. Since he was a pioneer evangelist, it may be that the subject of financial support was never introduced. They apparently did not discuss it, and Paul determined that he would not bring up the topic.

2. He placed no burden upon them (11:9)

When he initially entered Corinth and began to preach, Paul had real financial needs ("wanted"). But he chose not to place his ministry under any obligation to any man or group ("I was chargeable to no man"). This gave him freedom to speak without the possibility of offending his benefactors.

When Silas and Timothy rejoined him, they brought from the Macedonian churches a special monetary gift that "supplied" his needs (Acts 18:5). Earlier on this missionary journey, the Philippians twice sent him money when he was laboring in Thessalonica (Phil. 4:15–16).

Paul chose not to be financially "burdensome" to the Corinthians, both in the past ("I kept") and in the present ("I keep"). This refusal was not unique to Corinth, for he followed the same policy in Thessalonica (I Thess. 2:5–9; II Thess. 3:6–9).

3. He boasted about his free preaching (11:10–12)

It was paradoxical that Paul boasted about his determination to preach without pay and that his critics looked upon it as a great sin. He knew, however, that he was doing what Christ wanted him to do ("as the truth of Christ is in me"). Thus, he would not permit any man to "stop" his boasting in this area. The word "stop" *(phragēsetai)* is used of damming rivers (Prov. 25:26), of barricading a road (Hosea 2:6), and of the shutting of sinners' mouths before a holy God (Rom. 3:19).

Paul did not want to be paid for what he had to do and what he loved to do (I Cor. 9:15–18). He wanted to "make the gospel of Christ without charge" (I Cor. 9:18).

His critics, however, charged that the apostle refused to take money from the Corinthians because he did not love them (11:11). Paul adamantly denied this lie. He held love within his heart for them, and so did God.

He planned to continue his policy of not taking money from the church at Corinth (11:12). He was going to be consistent in his financial policy ("what I do, that I will do"). His purpose was to frustrate the Judaizers. They wanted Paul to take money so that they could compare honorariums and thereby compare the effectiveness of their respective ministries. Paul refused to be equated with them on the basis of their self-constructed standards ("that I may cut off occasion from them which desire occasion"). Rather, he intended that the comparisons be made on the basis of his standards ("they may be found even as we").

He desired to glory in what God had done through his ministry. He welcomed a comparison in achievement. He wanted them to see what he had done and what he had suffered for Christ.

II. HIS CONTRAST WITH THE FALSE TEACHERS (11:13–29)

Throughout the epistle, the opposition of the Judaizers has formed the background for the apostle's comments. No matter what he did, Paul had to defend himself against their attacks. Now, Paul staged a counteroffensive. He planned to unmask these critics publicly before the entire church.

A. Description of the False Teachers (11:13–15)

Jesus warned His generation about false prophets who would come as wolves in sheep's clothing (Matt. 7:15). Paul likewise cautioned the church about the inroads of grievous wolves who would not spare the flock of God's people (Acts 20:29).

1. Their Characteristics (11:13)

Three descriptive phrases are listed. *First,* they were "false apostles." They claim to have been sent by God, but they were not. The Bible speaks also about false christs (Mark 13:22), false prophets (Mark 13:22), false teachers (II Peter 2:1), and false brethren (11:26; Gal. 2:4). These Judaizers fit into every one of these categories. Christ commended the Ephesians because they "tried them which say they are apostles, and are not, and hast found them liars" (Rev. 2:2). Paul urged the Corinthians to examine these self-acclaimed apostles in the same way (cf. Rom. 16:17–18; Titus 1:10–16).

Second, they were "deceitful workers." The word "deceitful" *(dolioi)* comes from a term used for a lure or a snare. These Judaizers worked, but they worked at trapping men into doctrinal and moral error. They "by good words and fair speeches deceive the hearts of the simple" (Rom. 16:18).

Third, they were "transforming themselves into the apostles of Christ." This word "transforming" *(metaschēmatizomenoi)* refers to a change of outward appearance only. Since most men (like the Corinthians) seldom look below the surface, they are easily taken in by those who appear to be spiritual but who really are religious exploiters (Phil. 3:17–19). Unfortunately, the Corinthian church had accepted the Judaizers as genuine apostles of Christ.

2. Their cause (11:14–15a)

Believers should not "marvel" at such religious misrepresentation. Error must counterfeit the truth to be accepted. Satan knows this; thus, he masquerades as "an angel of light." His original goal was to be like God, not unlike Him (Isa. 14:12–14).

Jesus asserted that the religious leaders of Israel were of their father, the devil (John 8:44). Likewise, Paul charged that these Judaizers were really Satan's "ministers." They were not sent by Christ, as they claimed, but they were commissioned by the devil. Satan was their master, and he had done a masterful job of deception by getting the church to accept them as genuine apostles of Christ.

They were "ministers of righteousness." They did not exhort people to sin; rather, they encouraged men to be holy and to trust in their own religious effort to gain heaven. Their preaching was in open contradiction to the basic premise that self-produced righteousness within men is rejected completely by God (Isa. 64:5; Rom. 3:10; 10:3; Phil 3:6–9).

3. Their cure (11:15b)

Solomon wrote: "There is a way which seemeth right unto a man, but the end thereof are the ways of death" (Prov. 14:12). Any righteous life devoid of the imputed righteousness of God will end up in hell. All ministers who teach that men can contribute to their own salvation are destined for perdition (Gal. 5:10; Phil. 3:19; II Tim. 3:1–9; 4:14; II Peter 2:1). Paul firmly asserted that these Judaizers were unsaved. In this section, the apostle moved from irony to direct, hard words about his enemies.

B. Standard of Comparison (11:16–23a)

Paul decided that to communicate a spiritual principle he would have to lower himself to a human standard. But this was difficult for him to do. He despised human, external comparisons, but he felt constrained to meet the Judaizers on their own terms.

1. Glorying in self (11:16–18)

Paul recognized the risk that he was about to take. He did not want his readers to think that he was a "fool" or unwise *(aphrona)* in his bragging (11:16). There was a chance that they might not perceive the real intent of his self-disclosures. Nevertheless, he still desired a fair hearing from them even if they viewed him as foolish ("otherwise"). He asked for their indulgence in his "little" boasting so that he could prove his point (cf. 11:1).

Earlier, he asserted that he did not walk or war according to fleshly methods (10:1–4). Rather, he followed the humble example of Christ. He had no confidence in his person or ability (Phil. 3:3). Whatever spiritual gifts he had, he knew that he had received them from God (I Cor. 4:7). Thus, he admitted that what he was about to write concerning himself was "not after the Lord." Boasting is not according to the divine standard or example. Paul knew that, and he wanted the Corinthians to recognize it also. He could, however, boast about more achievements than could the critics. The "confidence" (literally, "foundation," *hupostasei)* of his boasting was a firm conviction that he was right, that he was in the will of God, and that his apostolic authority and message came directly from Christ.

Since his enemies gloried "after the flesh," Paul decided that he would place himself in that category where men compare themselves (11:18; cf. 10:12). Internally, he was superior to the best of the Judaizers (11:5). Now, he wanted the church to see that he was also better outwardly. On another occasion, the apostle followed the same procedure (Phil. 3:1–9). He claimed that, if anyone could get to heaven by his racial position or religious fervor, he would be that person: "If any other man thinketh that he hath whereof he might trust in the flesh, I more" (Phil. 3:4). Thus, Paul reluctantly did testify or "brag" about his many accomplishments to get across a basic spiritual truth.

2. *Impressing the church (11:19–20)*

The church was impressed with ministers who bragged about what they had done ("ye suffer fools gladly").[6] They were fascinated by the social, economic, and financial backgrounds of their speakers (11:22–23; cf. I Cor. 1:26–31). With a touch of irony, he mentioned that they

6. The word for "suffer" *(anechō*; 11:19–20) is the same as that translated earlier as "bear" (11:1, 4).

were wise and yet they gladly listened to those who were unwise. They were like college professors sitting enthralled at the feet of high school dropouts.

The church willingly submitted itself to those with whom it was impressed (11:20). They were awed by strong, authoritative personalities, not by humble servants. In appearance, the Judaizers were like the former and the apostle like the latter.

With sarcasm, Paul pointed out five ways in which they were impressed with religious braggarts and tyrants.[7] *First,* the Judaizers had enslaved them ("bring you into bondage"). They determined to make the church obedient to them. They wanted to force the church to accept circumcision and legalism as the basis of justification (cf. Gal. 2:4; 5:1; 6:12–13).

Second, they exploited the church ("devour you") for religious and material gain. They were like the scribes and Pharisees who devoured widows' houses (Luke 20:47).

Third, they took from the church, but never gave anything in return ("take of you"). They were like crafty fishermen catching fish for their own food and profit (cf. Luke 5:5; Rom. 16:18).

Fourth, they exalted themselves over the church ("exalt himself"). They acted like dictators, lords, or executives. They viewed themselves as superior. They wanted other church members to wash their feet. Their arrogance violated the revealed qualifications of humility and altruism for the ministry (Matt. 20:25–28; John 13:14–17; I Peter 5:1–3).

Fifth, they insulted the church ("smite you on the face"). They humiliated it. This action is the ultimate

7. Note the fivefold usage of "if." Since each conditional clause uses the indicative mood, Paul was describing what actually was taking place.

symbol of disrespect (cf. I Kings 22:24; Acts 23:2). Although believers should take such indignity in their identification with Christ (Luke 22:64), they must also recognize that the smiters are unspiritual. A godly pastor will not be a "striker" (I Tim. 3:3; Titus 1:7). There is a real difference between smiting on the cheek and spanking with the rod of chastisement.

3. Credentials (11:21–23a)

The Judaizers viewed Paul as having "reproach" (literally, "no honor," *atimian)* and being "weak" (11:21a; cf. 10:10). In their opinion, he did not have apostolic authority; if he did, he would have quelled the insurrection with force. Paul admitted that he was too weak to do what the false apostles had done to them (11:20). If honor involves arrogant tyranny, he did not want to have any.

Earlier, Paul repudiated the audacious boldness of those who compared themselves (10:12).[8] Now, in his "foolishness," he stood ready to compare his credentials with those of his critics ("I am bold also," 11:21b).

Paul came from Tarsus, an important city in Cilicia (Acts 21:39). He had the same racial background as the Judaizers. He was a Hebrew, an Israelite, a real physical descendant of Abraham (Rom. 9:1–5; 11:1; Phil 3:5). He had genealogical tables to support his claim.

To prove his point, he admitted that the Judaizers were "ministers of Christ" outwardly (11:23a). He was not only a minister, but a real apostle ("I am more"). Actually, he believed that they were apostate ministers of Satan (11:13–15).

8. The words "am bold" and "dare" are the same in the Greek *(tolmaō).*

An arch from the ancient wall at Tarsus.

C. Superiority of His Sufferings (11:23b–29)

Paul suffered "more" for Christ in the performance of his ministerial responsibilities than did his critics. In fact, there are indications that they never suffered for their false message (Gal. 6:12). In this passage, he disclosed features about his life and ministry that are not seen elsewhere in Scripture. He not only gloried in what he did, but also in what it cost him to do it. This section impresses the reader with all that Paul was able to do for God in the midst of such difficulty. It was a real triumph for Paul just to survive.

1. In direct persecutions (11:23b–25)

When Christ commissioned Paul to be an apostle, He said: "I will show him how great things he must suffer for my name's sake" (Acts 9:16). In these verses, Paul listed nine areas in which he experienced more persecution than any other minister. *First,* the abundant "labors" mean that he suffered more because he did more. Through his vigorous missionary activity, he became very fatigued from the hostility of satanically influenced men. *Second,* his body bore the scars and welts of excessive "stripes," beatings of all types (cf. Gal. 6:17). *Third,* he spent much time "in prisons." Before the writing of this book, only one imprisonment is recorded (Acts 16:23). Since the plural ("prisons") is used, there must have been others. At least four more occurred after the writing of this book: at Jerusalem (Acts 21:33); at Caeserea (Acts 24:27), and twice at Rome (Acts 28:16; II Tim. 4:16–17). *Fourth,* he was often exposed to the possibility of "death." He was left for dead at Lystra (Acts 14:19) and sentenced to death at Ephesus (1:8–10).

In the next listing he moved from the general to the specific. *Fifth,* he was whipped by the Jews on five separate occasions (11:24). Under the Mosaic law, no Jew could be beaten more than forty times in one whipping (Deut. 25:1–3); thus, they stopped at thirty-nine to avoid breaking the law. *Sixth,* he was beaten "with rods" three times by Gentile oppressors. Although Roman citizens were exempt, apart from a formal trial, Paul voluntarily submitted to such abuse (Acts 16:22; I Thess. 2:2). *Seventh,* he was "stoned" once at Lystra (Acts 14:19). *Eighth,* he "suffered shipwreck" three times, probably during flight from his persecutors. *Ninth,* twice the ships ran aground but once it broke apart in the sea. At that time, he had to keep himself afloat for a calendar day.

2. *In perils (11:26)*

And travel was hazardous. Because Paul moved about so much, he was often subject to the hardships of the first-century traveler. Nine such perils are listed: the weariness of "journeyings" without the comforts of home; the problem of crossing flooding rivers ("waters"); "robbers" who mugged travelers who came their way; the ostracism and persecution of his fellow Jews (I Thess. 2:15); the hatred and threats of Gentiles ("heathen"); and the problems connected with living conditions within the city, wilderness, or on the sea. His worst peril came from the "false brethren" who constantly harassed him.

3. In physical deprivation (11:27)

Paul was tired and sore at the end of each day ("weariness and painfulness," cf. I Thess. 2:9). He apparently seldom rested. The term "watchings" mean that he stayed up when he should have been asleep. This sleeplessness could have been caused by his manual labor, by spiritual preparation, by pain within his body, or by imminent threats upon his life.

He often had little food or drink to satisfy the needs of his body ("hunger and thirst"). There were times when he had no food at all ("fastings"). These periods of fasting do not seem to be voluntary and religious; rather, they were imposed upon him. He found himself "in cold and nakedness," often without suitable clothing and heated lodging. Is it any wonder that he did not look much like an official apostle of the church?

4. In care for the churches (11:28)

The outside pressures upon the apostle were enormous ("those things that are without"). The inner concerns were even greater in magnitude. Everyday he prayed for the converts and the churches established under his ministry. He kept in frequent contact by personal visits, correspondence, and sending his associates. Whenever these churches had problems, they appealed to Paul for solutions and help. This routine occurred "daily."

He pastored not just one church, but many flocks of believers. He wept and rejoiced over them. And yet, he never experienced an emotional or a mental breakdown.

5. *In personal criticism (11:29)*

Paul identified with his spiritual children. When they hurt, he hurt ("weak"). When someone attacked his converts, he burned with inner emotion. He wanted to stop these "wolves" who would ravage his spiritual lambs. He could not rest until his converts were morally and doctrinally safe.

How then could the church find fault with him, especially for refusing to take their money? How petty they seem when their criticism is compared with all that Paul did!

QUESTIONS FOR DISCUSSION

1. How does Satan corrupt the minds of believers today? How "simple" should biblical Christianity be in a sophisticated world?

2. In what ways are another Jesus and another gospel being preached today? Why are believers often deceived by these false teachers?

3. Why are churches more impressed with how a man preaches than with what he proclaims? Is pulpit oratory a form of outward appearance?

4. How can we distinguish between glorifying God and bragging in testimony meetings?

5. In what ways do ministers speak foolishly today? What kind of a mentality is impressed by self-acclaim?

6. Based upon outward appearances, do you think that your church would be interested in Paul as a candidate for

your pulpit? List the qualifications of a pastor in order of importance.

7. Should Christians in our nation suffer more for their faith today? Why are the lives of American Christians so different from that of Paul?

12

The Glory of Paul's Sufferings

II Corinthians 11:30—12:13

Paul ended this major section on the defense of his apostleship with a strong appeal to the authenticating value of his sufferings. He began this letter with a discussion of the necessity of sufferings in the believer's life (1:3–11; cf. Phil. 1:29). Certain spiritual lessons can be learned only in the crucible of physical trials. Thus, the apostle gloried in what he had suffered and in what he had learned.

I. SUFFERINGS AND BOASTING (11:30–33)

Most men brag about their heritage, their mental or athletic abilities, or their influential position in life. Although some boast about their endurance of physical ailments, rarely does anyone glory in the suffering itself.

A. Basis of His Boasting (11:30–31)

Because of the awkward predicament in Corinth, Paul was compelled to glory in or brag about his spiritual achievements (cf. 12:11). The situation demanded a radical, innovative solution. He wrote: "If I must needs glory." If it was necessary for him to boast, and it was, he determined that he would glory in those areas that he selected, not in those that the Judaizers had arbitrarily assigned to him.

Therefore, he boasted: "I will glory of the things which concern mine infirmities." He gloried both in what he suffered (12:10) and in why he suffered ("the things which concern"). To glory only in the beatings *per se* would be morbid; but to boast in the divine reasons behind the whippings is to experience satisfaction and victory. For the most part, he had just enumerated his infirmities (11:23–27), but he discussed them again later in the letter (12:7–10).

He appealed to God for divine corroboration of his testimony (11:31). Just as much of the world refused to believe the horrors of the Jewish holocaust during World War II, so Paul knew that some of his readers would view his list of hardships as fictional. There were few human witnesses to his multiple sufferings. The Judaizers, doubtlessly, would have charged him with a devious attempt to promote sympathy for himself.

After all he suffered, Paul could still identify his God and Father as "blessed" (cf. 1:3). His hardships did not make him bitter or rebellious; rather, they made him more loving and sympathetic toward people and their needs.

Paul emphatically wrote: "God knoweth that I lie not." God, who sees everything, saw what happened, why it occurred, and how the apostle responded. This was the second time in this epistle that Paul took a solemn oath before God to support the veracity of his testimony (cf. 1:23). He denied that he lied or exaggerated the truth.[1] The Judaizers were false or lying apostles (11:13), but what he said about himself was true. If there is lying, there

1. The usage of the present tense *pseudomai* ("I lie not") shows that lying was not part of his daily behavior.

can be no genuine fellowship with God or with Christ (I John 1:5–10).

B. Example of His Boasting (11:32–33)

Paul, of course, avoided persecution whenever possible. He was not afraid of it, but neither did he go out of his way to make it easier for his tormentors. His dramatic escape from Damascus simply reinforced the premise that he could have suffered far more if it had been God's will.

Why did Paul record this particular event? *First,* it marked the first time that there was a deliberate attempt to kill him because he was preaching the gospel. This experience occurred shortly after his conversion on the

The entrance to the house of Ananias in Damascus.

road to Damascus (Acts 9:1–9), his formal induction into the ministry (Acts 9:10–19), and his first public witness for Christ (Acts 9:20–22). The plot to assassinate him was led by the furious Jews with the assistance of the civil governor (11:32; cf. Acts 9:23–25). The term "Aretas" was the title for Arabian kings who ruled Nabatea, the region between the Red Sea and the Euphrates River, from 9 B.C.–A.D. 40.[2] Thus, at the very outset, his persecution came from both Jews and Gentiles and from both religious and political opponents. His subsequent sufferings could therefore be traced to this notable beginning.

Second, it dramatically illustrated the contrast between his human weakness and inability with the triumphant provision and sufficiency of a wise God. Would there be anything more humiliating than to be lowered in a basket out of a window by the hands of others? In that moment while he was in midair, there was nothing that he could do for himself. He had to trust completely in divine providence.

II. SUFFERINGS AND REVELATIONS (12:1–10)

Knowledge and suffering are not mutually exclusive. In this life, men often suffer for what they do not know. Paul, however, suffered for what he knew and whom he knew. Like John, he was persecuted "for the word of God and for the testimony of Jesus Christ" (Rev. 1:9). Contrariwise, although the Judaizers claimed that they knew the truth, they never suffered for that knowledge.

A. Revelations Before Sufferings (12:1–6)

Paul found it difficult to describe his sufferings to others. He felt foolish in doing it. It was even harder for

2. It is somewhat equivalent to the title "Pharaoh," used for the many kings of Egypt.

him to communicate what he privately knew about God. He knew that he had to go on with his comparative boasting even though it was not spiritually "expedient" (12:1a). He normally did not do what was not expedient (I Cor. 6:12; 10:23). But the pressure of the Judaizers upon the church forced him to suspend his policy.

1. His exaltation (12:1b–4)

Paul hastened to center his glorying in "visions and revelations of the Lord" (12:1b). The term "visions" *(optasias)* refers to what is seen, whereas the word "revelations" *(apokalupseis)* points to what is heard. He both saw and heard the risen Christ and what the Lord revealed to him. He saw the glorified Savior on the road to Damascus (Acts 9:3–9; 22:6–11; I Cor. 15:8), at Corinth (Acts 18:9–10), at Jerusalem (Acts 22:17–21), and probably in Arabia (Gal. 1:17). On other occasions, he saw the man of Macedonia in a vision (Acts 16:9) and an angel during his voyage to Rome (Acts 27:23–24).

Much of what he said and wrote came to him by direct revelation from Christ: the ordinance of the Lord's Supper (I Cor. 11:23); the gospel message of Christ's death and resurrection (I Cor. 15:3); and the distinctives of this church age (Eph. 3:3). He could say: "For I neither received [the gospel] of man, neither was I taught it, but by the revelation of Jesus Christ" (Gal. 1:12). He saw and heard what no Judaizer had ever witnessed.

In the next three verses (12:2–4), he related a specific supernatural event from his past. Hughes observed that this "was probably the most intimate and sacred of all Paul's religious experiences as a Christian."[3] His embarrassment

3. Philip E. Hughes, *Paul's Second Epistle to the Corinthians,* New International Commentary on the New Testament (Wm. B. Eerdmans Publishing Co., 1962), p. 428.

at this disclosure forced him to refer to himself anonymously ("I knew a man in Christ," 12:2a, 3).

Four key facts are enumerated about this unusual event. *First,* it occurred about "fourteen years" before the writing of this epistle (12:2). Since Paul composed the letter in Macedonia during the end of his third journey (A.D. 55), this would place the experience at a time before his missionary ministry began (Acts 13; A.D. 47).[4] It could have occurred while he was in Arabia (Gal. 1:17), or in Tarsus (Acts 9:30), or in Antioch (Acts 11:26). It could not, however, refer to his conversion, because that happened even before the fourteen years limit and because Paul often referred to the supernatural circumstances surrounding his conversion. Also, it could not refer to his stoning and possible death at Lystra, since that event took place just eight years before (Acts 14:19).

Second, he did not know whether he had the experience "in the body" or "out of the body" (12:2–3). The real self or ego is centered in the immaterial part of man, the soul or the spirit. The event was real, personal, and memorable. He did not know whether he was in his natural body at the time, but God knew. If it was "in the body," then his body was miraculously transported from earth to heaven. The deacon–evangelist Philip was "caught away" bodily by the Holy Spirit and transferred from Gaza to Azotus (Acts 8:39–40). If it was "out of the body," then he was removed from the physical organism and entered into a spiritual state to pass through the heavens. Both Ezekiel and John had similar experiences (Ezek. 3:12–15; Rev. 1:10; 4:1–2).

4. Tasker dates it one or two years before his first missionary journey began. R.V.G. Tasker, *The Second Epistle of Paul to the Corinthians,* Tyndale New Testament Commentaries (Grand Rapids: Wm. B. Eerdmans Publishing Co., 1960), p. 172.

Third, he was caught up into "the third heaven" or "paradise" (12:2, 4). There are three heavens mentioned in the Scripture: the atmospheric heavens that surround the earth (Deut. 11:11); the second heaven that contains the sun, moon, and stars (Gen. 1:14); and the third heaven, or the presence of God (Isa. 63:15). When the resurrected Christ ascended to the right hand of the Father, He passed through the heavens (plural, indicating first and second; Heb. 4:14). The word "paradise" comes from a Persian term meaning "a park." It is used in the Septuagint for the Garden of Eden.[5] When Christ and the repentant thief died, they both went into paradise, the place of comfort within Hades (Luke 16:22; 23:43; Acts 2:27–31). Through His resurrection and ascension, Christ transported all believers from the paradise of Hades to the paradise of the third heaven (Eph. 4:8–10; Heb. 12:22–24). Therefore the only "paradise" in existence today is in the third heaven. All believers upon their deaths go there to be with Christ (5:6–8; Phil 1:23).

Fourth, he "heard unspeakable words, which it is not lawful for a man to utter" (12:4). He must have seen and heard things that were not inscripturated until later (e.g., the holy city, Rev. 21:22). Did he hear words spoken by God or by angels or by both? Did he hear what does not pertain to the redemptive program of this present time-space universe? It is vain, however, to speculate about such questions (Titus 3:9). Whatever he heard, no man before or after Paul has heard it. His experience was unique.

2. *His reservation (12:5–6)*

The Judaizers had no inhibitions about boasting. To impress their audiences they told everything that they

5. The Septuagint is the Greek translation of the Hebrew Old Testament.

could, and then some more. As much as Paul tried to insert himself into their standard of glorying, he constantly restrained himself. He could not boast enthusiastically as they did.

If some other Christians had the heavenly experience that the apostle enjoyed, they would have mentioned it frequently. They would have welcomed the adulation of fellow Christians. Not so with Paul. In modesty he chose to use it anonymously ("of such an one will I glory," 12:5a).

When Paul decided to use his own name in boasting, he directed it toward his sufferings. He said: ". . . yet of myself I will not glory, but in mine infirmities" (12:5b; cf. 11:30).

The "desire to glory" was within his human nature (12:6a). People naturally like to brag about what they know, where they have traveled, and whom they have seen. When that desire is dominated by the sin principle, however, the bragging of men becomes obnoxious. When it is controlled by the Holy Spirit, then the witness of yielded believers to the works of God can be a blessing to others. Throughout, Paul restrained himself: "I shall not be a fool." In one sense, he was willing to be foolish when he discussed his sufferings, but he did not want to be foolish in the disclosure of private, ecstatic experiences.

What he said was true. There was much more that he could say about his heavenly vision, but he decided against it ("for I will say the truth: but now I forbear"). Most believers either say not enough or too much about what God has done in their lives. Paul knew what to say, how much to say, and when to stop.

In this report, he did not want to act contrary to what the Corinthians knew about him ("lest any man should think of me"). When Paul lived among them for almost two years, they never observed in his behavior any signs of self-exaltation ("above that which he seeth me to be"). When others talked to the church about Paul (e.g., Titus, Timothy, Apollos), they never intimated that there was a sense of bragging resident within the apostle ("or that he heareth of me").

B. Sufferings After Revelations (12:7–10)

People can well heed the warning that "knowledge puffeth up" (I Cor. 8:1). It is presumptuous for believers to be proud about what they know. When their finite perception is compared with infinite, divine omniscience, they must surely be ashamed (I Cor. 8:2–3). Knowledge apart from the control of compassionate, humble love is self-destructive.

1. His humiliation (12:7)

Paul admitted that within himself "dwelleth no good thing" (Rom. 7:18). Even as a redeemed sinner, the urge to feel proud was present in his life. Thus, he felt the need to be humbled by God "lest [he] should be exalted above measure through the abundance of the revelations." In spiritual hindsight, he could see how the wisdom of God manifested itself through his physical weakness. When a believer thinks that he knows more than most others, he should be reminded that he is still a creature. In the apostle's case, the affliction served as a preventative ("lest").

The means of humiliation was "a thorn in the flesh, the messenger of Satan to buffet" him. The word "thorn" *(skolops)* can refer to an actual thorn, splinter, or stake. But it was not something that could be removed with a tweezers or by surgery.

It was "in the flesh."[6] From the context, it appears to be a serious physical ailment (12:5, 9–10). It has been identified variously as malaria, partial blindness (cf. Gal. 4:13–15), epilepsy, insomnia, or severe migraine headaches. Some, however, including the Reformers, saw it as a "spiritual" thorn. Just as the Canaanites were a thorn in the side of Israel (Num. 33:55), so the Jews or the Judaizers could have personified the thorn for Paul. Even specific individuals, such as Alexander (II Tim. 4:14) or Hymaneus and Philetus (II Tim. 2:17), have been suggested. The former view, however, seems to be more plausible.

It was also called the "messenger of Satan." Satan has been given permission by God to afflict the saints (Job 1–2; Luke 22:31). Paul interpreted this trial to be from God ("was given"). It was designed to curtail his pride and promote humble submissiveness. The buffeting was constant (cf. Matt. 26:67; I Cor. 4:11), but the intensity increased at various intervals.

2. His intercession (12:8)

Although it was a messenger of Satan, he knew that it had come ultimately from God. If God had given it, then God could take it away. On three separate occasions he asked the Lord for its permanent removal.[7] Since he did not pray continually, this fact might indicate that his ailment or pain was not constant. Whenever it attacked him, he prayed for its removal.

This event demonstrates that sickness is not always the chastisement of God for personal acts of sin (I Cor.

6. The phrase *tēi sarki* can be either locative ("in the flesh") or dative ("with reference to the flesh").

7. The verb is in the aorist subjunctive. The subject of the verb can be either "it" ("thorn") or "he" ("messenger").

11:30). Rather, it may serve to prevent sin. Also, it shows that it is not always the will of God to heal, even to heal the most spiritual believer.

3. His submission (12:9–10)

After three requests and three denials, God directly spoke to Paul: "My grace is sufficient for thee: for my strength is made perfect in weakness" (12:9a). God wanted the apostle to keep the thorn. It was one way by which he could learn to trust God more. The grace of God not only saves, it also sustains. It is abundant and available for the daily needs of believers (John 1:16). The strength ("ability," *dunamis)* of God achieves its goal or is finalized through human weakness. This is true of salvation: "For when we were yet without strength, in due time Christ died for the ungodly" (Rom. 5:6). It is also true of service. When a believer is physically weak, he must depend upon the ability of God to accomplish his tasks.

When Paul learned the truth of that divine revelation, he changed his attitude regarding his affliction from prayer to praise (12:9b). He stopped asking God to remove the thorn and, instead, he thanked Him for it. He did not just endure the ailment, but he "gladly" gloried in it. He then gloried in all of his infirmities (note the switch from the singular "thorn" to the plural "infirmities"). Above all things, he wanted the power of Christ to "rest" upon him. The word "rest" *(episkēnōsēi)* literally means "may pitch his tent." Paul wanted to be enveloped by the ability of God. If it meant that he must endure infirmities to attain such power, then he was willing that the infirmities remain.

Paul was not asking anyone to feel sorry for him just because he suffered so much. Rather, he "took pleasure" *(eudokō)* in all of the hardships that he endured "for

Christ's sake." He gladly suffered as a Christian (I Peter 4:16). Five types of physical difficulties are listed.

The reason for such spiritual pleasure is paradoxical: "for when I am weak, then am I strong." He was not strong in his own strength, but in divine strength.[8] The reverse is doubtless true. When a believer is physically strong, he may not rely upon God as much and thus become spiritually weak. Spiritual, inner power is far more important than physical, outward health.

III. SUFFERINGS AND APOSTLESHIP (12:11–13)

In this major section, Paul summarized the defense of his apostleship.

A. His Seal (12:11)

Again, he admitted that he had "become a fool in glorying" (cf. 11:1, 16). He had acted contrary to his principles and reputation. Perhaps, what he had written about himself might later be used against him.[9]

They had "compelled" him to write such personal data in his own defense. They forced him, which made it absolutely necessary. He had to do it against his better judgment. He just wanted them to know that basic fact.

If they would have defended him against the Judaizers and the dissident minority, he would not have needed to glory in his sufferings or in his revelations. As the beneficiaries of his ministry, they should have commended him.

He claimed to be equal to any of the Judaizers, "the very chiefest apostles." He could say this even on the basis

8. The words "strength," "power," and "strong" all come from the same Greek word.

9. The perfect tense *gegona* ("I am become") stresses the existing results of a completed action. What results would stem from these two chapters?

of outward appearance and the comparison of ministries. He claimed earlier, however, that they were false apostles, sent by Satan.

In position, he was "something," but in person, he was "nothing." After boasting about all that he did, he remained aware that he was what he was by the grace of God (I Cor. 15:10). He saw himself as the "least of the saints" (Eph. 3:8) and the "chief" of sinners (I Tim. 1:15).

B. His Signs (12:12)

The ministry of Jesus Christ was divinely authenticated by signs (John 20:30–31). He pointed to His works as a proof that He was sent by the Father (John 5:36; 10:37–38). When He commissioned the apostles, He gave them power to perform similar signs (Matt. 10:7–8; Mark 16:15–20). With reference to the apostles, the Book of Hebrews states that God was "bearing them witness, both with signs and wonders, and with divers miracles, and gifts of the Holy Ghost, according to his own will" (Heb. 2:4).[10]

Paul performed such signs in their midst when he originally evangelized the city. That fact in itself should have proved the reality of his apostleship. They were also done "in all patience." This word does not refer to a characteristic of a sign, but it points out the difficult circumstances in which they were demonstrated.

The three descriptive words do not indicate three different types of signs, but rather three various features of the same sign.[11] The term "signs" *(sēmeiois)* emphasizes the spiritually instructive value of the miracle. The word "wonders" *(terasi)* looks at the awe and amazement

10. The same three words for signs in this verse are found in 12:12.

11. Only one preposition *(en)* is used with the series of words.

created within the observers. The third characteristic, "deeds" *(dunamesi),* stresses the power of God exhibited in the miracle.

C. His Sin (12:13)

The only "wrong" that Paul had committed against the church was his refusal to take money from them. For this reason, the church developed an "inferiority" complex. The church felt degraded because Paul had taken money from other churches but not from them (cf. 11:7–9). The irony of the situation is that they had failed to give to the welfare collection at the same time they were protesting the apostle's financial policy.

Sin must be confessed for fellowship to be restored. Paul wanted to be reconciled to the church, so he ironically confessed: ". . . forgive me this wrong." If that were the only barrier between them, he wanted their forgiveness.

QUESTIONS FOR DISCUSSION

1. Are there genuine visions and revelations today? How do you respond to those who claim to have spiritual dreams, to have seen angels, or to have seen Christ?

2. Discuss some events in your life that were both natural and miraculous (cf. 11:32–33). How can you testify to others that your deliverance was providential and not coincidental?

3. Do believers brag today about their knowledge? Do you know Christians who brag about their ignorance? Is there any justification for such boasting?

4. How can the purposes of infirmities be discerned? When do they come as chastisement? As preventatives? As trials?

5. Does God heal today? Are there genuine faith healers today? When should a believer stop praying for physical healing?

6. Do some believers endure infirmities rather than take pleasure in them? What is the difference? What can be done to grow spiritually in this area?

7. Are real apostles in existence today? Are there any outward proofs for such claims? If the gift of apostleship ceased in the first century, how can it be demonstrated?

13

The Preparations for Paul's Visit

II Corinthians 12:14—13:14

The final portion of the epistle deals with Paul's proposed visit to Corinth. Now that a revival had erupted, there was no reason to delay his coming any longer. Thus, he exclaimed: "Behold, the third time I am ready to come to you" (12:14a).

The mention of the adjective "third" implies that there were two prior visits.[1] The first, of course, was the original evangelization of the city during his second missionary journey (Acts 18:1–18). This third visit actually occurred at the end of his third journey (Acts 20:2). No second journey, however, was recorded by Luke in the Book of Acts. It is logical to date it during his three years of ministry at Ephesus (Acts 19:1–41; 20:31). After he wrote the first epistle, he may have deemed it necessary to make a trip across the Aegean to deal with the rebels who had refused to submit to the authority of the first letter (cf. I Cor. 4:18–21). This trip ended in disappointment (2:1; 12:21). The atmosphere at Corinth was different now, caused by the painful letter (2:4; 7:8) and by the effective

1. Several commentators, however, believe that the word "third" refers only to three preparations for a visit. The second was canceled because of the rebellion in the church (1:15–17).

ministry of Titus. He was now "ready" to move from Macedonia into Achaia (Acts 20:2).

I. HIS ATTITUDE IN COMING (12:14–21)

In the first epistle, he placed the burden of his coming upon them: "What will ye? shall I come unto you with a rod, or in love, and in the spirit of meekness?" (I Cor. 4:21). His attitude was conditioned by their attitude. In his desire to achieve maximum effectiveness of ministry, he adapted himself and his methods to the circumstances (I Cor. 9:19–22).

A. No Outward Exploitation (12:14–18)

1. He would again refuse their money (12:14)

He planned to remain consistent in his financial policy. He had not been "burdensome" in the past (11:9; 12:13) and he would not be in the future. It would have been very easy for him to have taken advantage of them. After all, they felt wronged that they had not contributed to his support. They doubtless would have given him a large love offering if he would have asked for one.

He then said: ". . . for I seek not your's but you." He wanted them, not their money. No value can be placed upon renewed affection between reconciled parties. He was interested in their spiritual welfare, not their material wealth.

He then justified his financial policy with an analogy from the typical home: ". . . for the children ought not to lay up for the parents, but the parents for the children" (12:14b). A parent should not expect to be paid for being a parent. Children are not to provide for the basic necessities of a home: food, clothing, and shelter. These are areas of responsibility belonging to parents. Since Paul was their spiritual parent, he wanted to give to them. Most parents do not want money in return for their effort; they only desire the love and gratitude of their children.

2. He planned to give himself to them (12:15)

In spite of all the heartache and the hardship caused by the ungrateful Corinthians, he "gladly" willed to "spend and be spent" for them. The verb "spend" *(dapanaō)* refers to the spending of money, time, and effort. For example, the woman with an issue of blood spent all her money in her attempt to find a cure (Mark 5:25). Paul was willing to give all that he had for them. He also was yielded enough to give himself completely ("to be spent").[2] Out of His great love, Christ not only gave us salvation, but He gave us Himself. Paul planned to do likewise.

What intensely hurt Paul was that as his love increased for the Corinthians, their love for him diminished. How sad it must have been for him to write: ". . . the more abundantly I love you, the less I be loved" (12:15b). The more he gave to them, the more unthankful they became. And yet, that did not stop him from loving them, just as parents keep on loving their ungrateful, rebellious children.

3. He desired reconciliation (12:16–18)

Their unloving and suspicious attitudes toward him did not force him to turn his back on them. He did not hold it against them. He put it all in the past ("But be it so;" literally, "let it be," *estō).* It did not compel him to approach them from an absolute, authoritative position, demanding their money for the welfare collection or for himself ("I did not burden you"). The Judaizers had charged that Paul was using the welfare fund as a pretense to get money for himself.

2. This verb is intensified by the addition of the prefix *ek (ekdapanaō).*

Although his methods were biblical and honest (4:2), he admitted that he used ingenious methods to win the Corinthians back to himself: ". . . nevertheless, being crafty, I caught you with guile" (12:16b). He criticized the Judaizers for being "deceitful" (same word as "guile"; *dolos).* Again, the word means to catch with bait or a snare. Paul caught them with Titus and his tearful letter. The "guile" can either be good or bad, depending upon its purpose. Once the revival had occurred in the church and in their hearts, he knew that this situation would be an opportune time to reintroduce the need for the collection. Thus, he did take advantage of their warmth toward him to get money for the needy saints in Jerusalem.

He did not, however, exploit them through any of his representatives (12:17). He did not take support money from them directly or indirectly through his associates. This was true in the past, and now it would also be true with the sending of Titus and the two brothers (12:18a).[3]

Titus did not make "a gain" of them when he was there in the midst of the revival. Like Paul, he was interested in them, not in their money. The apostle's life and motivation were mirrored in his associate: ". . . walked we not in the same spirit? walked we not in the same steps?" (12:18b). They were both loving and giving men. They were both controlled by the Holy Spirit. They walked in the same "spirit and steps" because they both were following Christ (I Cor. 11:1).

B. Much Inward Apprehension (12:19–21)

In his ministry, the apostle was both optimistic and realistic (2:14). Pessimism never overtook him, although he

3. The usage of the singular "brother" may indicate that one of the three was supported by other churches in the endeavor (8:16–24; cf. 8:19).

did admit to human fears and weaknesses (7:5). Thus, as he anticipated his visit to Corinth, he wondered what would actually happen when he arrived.

1. Possibility of more defense (12:19)

The opening question implies that the church might expect him to further defend his integrity, ministry, and financial policy when he was in their midst.[4] The word "excuse" means a "reasoned defense" *(apologoumetha;* transliterated "apologize"). There was nothing more that could be said. If they were not convinced by the second epistle, they would never be sure of Paul's honesty.

His speaking had its source in "God" and was centered "in Christ." His written defense, although very human and emotional in character, was inspired of God (II Tim. 3:16; II Peter 1:20–21). His words were divine words.

He loved them and desired their "edifying" most of all (cf. 10:8). If they expected him to vindicate himself, they were wrong. He was coming to build them up.

2. Fear of their real spiritual condition (12:20)

With straightforwardness, he confessed: "I fear." He still had some lingering misgivings about the total effects of the revival. Was it temporary and superficial or was it permanent and genuine? Did Titus see deeply enough into their hearts? Was the situation as great as Titus pictured it? With all candor, he itemized three fears.

First, he was afraid that their spiritual life would not be where he wanted it to be ("I shall not find you such as I would"). He wanted them to manifest holy characteristics, even the fruit of the Spirit. Sometimes, disobedient chil-

4. The sentence can also be viewed as declarative: "Ye are again thinking that we are excusing ourselves unto you."

dren will obey, but apart from love. Paul would not be content with outward conformity marked by inward coldness.

Second, he was afraid that he would have to exercise his authority in a way they would not like ("and that I shall be found unto you such as ye would not"). He wanted to be received as a forgiving father by repentant children. If the revival were only superficial, then he would appear as the stern disciplinarian.

Third, he was afraid that personal differences had not yet been settled. These eight listed sins served to divide the church internally (I Cor. 1:11) and to divorce it from the apostle. They were: "debates" or contentions (I Cor. 1:11, same word); "envyings" or personal jealousy; "wraths" or fits of temper; "strifes" or divisions into cliques; "backbitings" or gossip spoken behind one's back; "whisperings" or defamations of character in the form of innuendo; "swellings" or the manifestation of pride; and "tumults" or vehement disagreement in public meetings.

3. *Renewal of humiliation (12:21)*

The usage of the negative "lest" shows that Paul feared or wondered how God would providentially control the delicate meeting. If he came into the church and found the unrepentant boldly seated before him, he knew that there was a possibility that he just might drop to his knees and weep over their hardness ("that I shall bewail many"). Instead of authoritatively reprimanding the sinners, he conjectured that God might "humble" him in their presence. Some supporters probably would want him to yell and to pound the pulpit to get his way, but the apostle knew that God might work through his loving heart in a far different way.

The sins listed all deal with sexual impurity. The term "fornication" refers to private promiscuity whereas "lasciviousness" points to public displays of indecency. Both manifest the general term of "uncleanness."

II. HIS AUTHORITY IN COMING (13:1–10)

In both epistles, Paul warned that he would use his apostolic authority to the fullest extent if the situation demanded it (10:10–11; I Cor. 4:18–21). Although he preferred to come into their midst as their spiritual father, he would not shrink from coming as *the* apostle to the Gentiles.

A. His Commitment to Discipline (13:1)

1. He would follow the biblical procedure (13:1)

The Mosaic Law taught that discipline could not be executed against an accused offender if there was only one witness (Deut. 19:15). There had to be corroborative evidence testified "in the mouth of two or three witnesses."

Jesus stated that the method for restoring an erring brother involved three major steps: personal confrontation, the support of two or three witnesses, and a hearing before the entire church (Matt. 18:15–17). Elsewhere, Paul wrote: "A man that is an heretic after the first and second admonition reject; knowing that he that is such is subverted, and sinneth, being condemned of himself" (Titus 3:10–11).

Paul thus equated his three visits with the required three witnesses. If they refused to repent and to submit to his authority, he then would have no choice but to discipline them.

2. He would not spare the sinner (13:2)

In one sense the first visit, to evangelize Corinth, could be construed as one witness in the procedure of discipline. Paul, however, may have equated the first witness with his short, painful trip ("I told you before," cf. 2:1). The second witness could then be part of the second epistle, to serve as his testimony *in absentia* ("and foretell you, as if I were present, the second time"). Thus his next arrival would constitute the third witness. Regardless, the rebels had at least two or three warnings to repent.

He specifically addressed two groups: "them which heretofore have sinned" (cf. 12:21) and "all other." The concept behind the verb ("have sinned") is that the effects of the past sins still remained and that there had been no restitution or correction of wrongs.[5] The phrase "all other" must include those influenced by the Judaizers.

He warned them that he would not "spare" them. This might involve deliverance to Satan for severe discipline (I Cor. 5:5; I Tim. 1:20).

3. He would manifest Christ's authority (13:3–4)

The critics claimed that Paul was weak before the church, but mighty away from the church (10:9–10). Thus, the church was eager to see a demonstration of authoritative speech from Paul. He knew that when he both spoke and wrote, Christ was "speaking" in and through him. He thus planned to give them a "proof," an outward display of his intrinsic authority.

The church recognized that the Head of the church, Jesus Christ, was "mighty" not "weak." Thus, they could not understand why His representative, namely Paul, would be weak and not mighty.

5. The verb is in the perfect tense: *proēmartēkosi* (also in 12:21).

The church had forgotten, however, that Christ manifested His weakness through humble obedience to the crucifixion. After that event he demonstrated His power through His resurrection (13:4a). It is also true that His first advent revealed His weakness but that His second advent will declare His power. At His first coming, He permitted men to humiliate Him, but at His second coming, He will subdue all of His enemies.

Since Paul was spiritually identified with Christ, he also had to manifest his weakness before showing his power: "For we also are weak in him, but we shall live with him by the power of God toward you" (13:4b). When he first went to correct the problems, he was humiliated. Now, at this next visit, he planned to demonstrate his apostolic authority.

B. His Challenge to Spirituality (13:5–10)

In a sense, Paul had been both his own character witness and defense attorney. The church was the jury. Now, he reversed the roles. They were on the witness stand, and he was the prosecuting attorney.

1. To be sure of their spiritual relationship (13:5)

They wanted a proof of his apostolic authority. Now he desired a proof of their salvation and of their sanctification.[6] Three pointed commands were aimed at them. *First,* "examine yourselves, whether ye be in the faith." They were to test their beliefs and their behavior to see whether they were really saved. Their resistance to his authority and their persistent sin could be marks of an unregenerate life (I John 3:6).

6. The verb "prove" and the noun "proof" (13:3) come from the same Greek root *(dokimazō).*

Second, "prove your own selves." Just as Paul had given proof of his apostolic authority and integrity, they were to do the same for their condition. Were they carnal or spiritual?

Third, "know . . . your own selves." The verb "know" *(epiginōskete)* stresses a thorough understanding of one's life and relationship to Christ. Was Christ "in" them? If not, then they were "reprobates" *(adokimoi),* a term that means "disapproved." It is just the opposite of "proved" (13:3). It could refer either to that they were not really saved or that their lives were useless before God (cf. I Cor. 9:27; same word as "castaway").

2. *To have confidence in Paul (13:6)*

Paul knew that he was saved and that he was an effective apostle. He strived not to be a reprobate, and he was successful (I Cor. 9:27). His ministerial usefulness had been questioned by the dissidents. If the Corinthians would obey the three commands precisely, then they would also have full understanding that he was genuine.

3. *To be holy (13:7)*

Paul prayed that they might not do anything that was "evil" *(kakon),* but that they might do what was "honest" (literally "good," *kalon).*

His purpose for his prayer was clear. He did not desire their obedience simply to make his ministry "appear approved." Rather, he wanted them to do what was right, although it might mean that he would be misunderstood and misrepresented again. If the dissidents would repent before he came, he would not need to manifest his apostolic authority. Nonetheless, an outward display of apostolic power was the very thing that would remove all doubts as to his apostleship.

Paul was not selfish. He would rather see them do the right thing than see himself exalted.

4. To be truthful (13:8)

In the long run, truth will win. Paul spoke the truth. He lived "for the truth." He wanted the church to recognize truth and to stand for it regardless of the opinions of others. He knew that God would vindicate the spiritually minded believers and himself. He once wrote: "For there must be also heresies among you, that they which are approved may be made manifest among you" (I Cor. 11:19).

5. To be perfect (13:9)

Paul was willing to keep his reputation as a "weak" apostle if it meant that they would deal with their rebellion before he came. Thus, they would be "strong." He wanted God to do a mighty work in their lives, and he preferred that it be done before he arrived.

More than anything, he prayed for their "perfection." This word is used for the repair of what is broken. He wanted the church to be put together again into a holy temple before God (I Cor. 1:10; 3:16).

6. To be edified (13:10)

The epistle basically ends with this summary of his fundamental proposition: Paul wanted to build up, not to tear down. Christ gave him "power," or authority *(exousian),* for the positive purpose of "edification," not for the negative goal of "destruction."

Thus he wrote this epistle to build them up in the faith. If they followed his directions, he then would not have to use "sharpness" when he arrived. It was now up to them. Did they want edification or destruction?

III. CLOSING REMARKS

A. Admonitions (13:11)

As he brought the epistle to a close, he acknowledged that both the church and he were "brethren" in Christ. Although he challenged the dissidents, he believed that the great majority of the church was saved.

Five quick commands are given. *First,* "farewell" (literally, "rejoice," *chairete).* They should rejoice in what they possessed in Christ and in what He had just done in their lives. *Second,* "be perfect." Again, he charged them to mend the broken hearts and the broken relationships that still existed among them. The divisive parties should again become one.

Third, "be of good comfort." They were to encourage, to exhort, and to comfort each other. Even after personal problems are resolved, the offenders can feel very depressed (cf. 2:7–8). *Fourth,* "be of one mind" (cf. I Cor. 1:10; Phil. 2:2; 4:2). They were to think the same things. They were to manifest the mind of Christ. *Fifth,* "live in peace." Believers should try "to keep the unity of the Spirit in the bond of peace" (Eph. 4:3). Personality differences and conflicts are bound to come, but when the peace of God rules in the hearts of believers, there will be forgiveness and forbearance (Col. 3:15).

For obedience, there are blessings forthcoming. Theirs would be the assurance of the nearness of the "God of love and peace." When believers draw close to God, they then will love each other more and will be at peace with each other.

B. Greetings (13:12–13)

Inner love should manifest itself publicly. If believers love each other, they will touch each other. In Jewish synagogues, men would kiss the men and the women would kiss other women. There was no exchange between the sexes. The early churches, both Jewish and Gentile, continued the custom. In our present day, this is still practiced by some congregations, although it has been replaced for the most part by shaking hands.

Paul then expressed greetings from "all the saints" in Macedonia.

C. Benediction (13:14)

The benediction included "grace," "love," and "communion." Those spiritual blessings originated from the three Persons of the trinitarian God: "Lord Jesus Christ," "God" (Father), and the "Holy Spirit." Since all three Persons are equal in divine essence, they can be listed in any order.

QUESTIONS FOR DISCUSSION

1. What principles for proper parent-child relationships can be gleaned from Paul's statements to the church? To what extent should parents "lay up" (provide) for their children?

2. Can we be more interested in what we can get from people than in people themselves? How does this take place in church? What can be done to correct it?

3. How can differences between people be better solved by tears than by yelling? Why do families break up? Can there be too much discipline in the home?

4. Are Christians guilty of judging people before there are two or three witnesses? What should be done about a believer who spreads falsehoods about another?

5. In what ways can a Christian be both weak and strong? When should he be weak? When should he be strong?

6. How should professing Christians examine their spiritual condition and relationships? How can reprobates be discerned?

7. Are believers more interested in their reputations than in genuine results? What can be done about this?

Selected Bibliography

Broomall, Wick. "The Second Epistle to the Corinthians," *The Wycliffe Bible Commentary.* Edited by Charles F. Pfeiffer and Everett F. Harrison. Chicago: Moody Press, 1963.

Hobbs, Herschel H. *The Epistles to the Corinthians.* Grand Rapids: Baker Book House, 1960.

Hodge, Charles. *An Exposition of the Second Epistle to the Corinthians.* Grand Rapids: Wm. B. Eerdmans Publishing Co., 1953.

Hughes, Philip Edgcumbe. *Paul's Second Epistle to the Corinthians.* New International Commentary on the New Testament. Grand Rapids: Wm. B. Eerdmans Publishing Co., 1962.

Ironside, H. A. *Addresses on the Second Epistle to the Corinthians.* New York: Loizeaux Bros., 1939.

Morgan, G. Campbell. *The Corinthian Letters of Paul.* Westwood, N.J.: Fleming H. Revell Co., 1956.

Moule, Handley C. G. *The Second Epistle to the Corinthians.* Grand Rapids: Zondervan Publishing House, 1962.

Plummer, Alfred. *A Critical and Exegetical Commentary on the Second Epistle of St. Paul to the Corinthians.* International Critical Commentary. Edinburgh: T. & T. Clark, 1956.

Robertson, Archibald Thomas. *Word Pictures in the New Testament,* vol. 4. Nashville: Broadman Press, 1931.

Tasker, R. V. G. *The Second Epistle of Paul to the Corinthians.* Tyndale New Testament Commentaries. Grand Rapids: Wm. B. Eerdmans Publishing Co., 1960.